INFLUENCER SECRETS

HOW TO BUILD YOUR SOCIAL MEDIA BRAND FAST

SMM PUBLISHING

CONTENTS

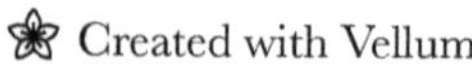 Created with Vellum

ABOUT THE BOOK

Are you passionate about something? It could be in any area of your interests at all. You might be passionate about fashion, travelling, cooking, or another topic, and you have been thinking of impacting and influencing people in this area? Here's all you need to start your journey toward becoming a noteworthy influencer.

The joy that comes with having a community of followers who trust you immensely is a priceless feeling. The satisfaction and fulfillment that comes from having a large group of people who count on your words is unbeatable.

You may be struggling with how to get your goal of being an influencer to reality; how exactly do you go about it? Rest assured that you will be fully equipped and completely ready after reading and taking the prescribed steps in this eBook. You might wonder how your favorite influencers have built their large fan base? "It's not easy," you say to yourself. "It would take years." for now, sit back, relax, and enjoy every bit of the information you really need to keep you on track. Cheers to becoming the impactful influencer you have always wanted to be!

CHAPTER ONE: EXPRESSING WITH PASSION

One very important human skill anyone can learn is the ability to communicate effectively, and more importantly, passionately. There are times we read a book, an article, or publication, and we just feel this burning urge within us; we can relate with whatever picture the writer is trying to create in our minds. Why do we cry when we read novels or watch movies? Why do we get really angry within our souls at characters who aren't even real? Have you ever felt like shredding a character to pieces after reading a book? This only happens when the person communicating with us does so passionately. This could be a writer, blogger, or even an influencer. Enthusiasm is contagious, and it's an effective way of getting people onto the same page as you. The ability to stir people's emotions is very important if you'll be communicating with a target audience. At some point or another, you will feel the need to express yourself in such a way that a strong impression is left in the mind of your audience. Nobody wants to be tagged as a boring conversationalist.

I personally know a community leader whose posts I look forward to reading every time. It is only because I can almost hear her voice when I read her posts. She communicates so passionately that I never forget whatever she talks about.

You must have heard a motivational speaker talk and have probably wondered at how they make people want to change their lives just by communicating in such an impressive manner. If you want to be a successful influencer, you must be able to impress people or create an impression—a positive one at that. Being an influencer has a lot to do with gaining the trust of your audience as well as their attention. In this chapter, you will learn how to communicate and express yourself with passion. You will learn how to make people recognize your voice, respect your ideas, and pay great attention to your content.

5 WAYS TO EXPRESS YOUR PASSION

Find your niche: Communicating effectively has a lot to do with finding your niche. Your first step toward becoming an influencer is knowing exactly what you want to talk about and to make sure you talk about it with passion. Your topic should be something you are very comfortable and familiar with. If you are talking about something you are enthusiastic about, people will feel your passion and see your originality. Leaving an impression in the mind of your audience requires in-depth content, and this can only be achieved when you stay within your niche. Know exactly what intrigues you and be confident enough so people see that you know quite a lot about what you are talking about. In the influencing world, people talk about practically every topic you can think of; nevertheless, you can still find your audience. If fashion is what catches your fancy, then you must make sure your content doesn't depart from that. That being said, you can only be passionate about what you love. Passion and enthusiasm are contagious, and this will show through in your content. While finding your niche, make sure it's not one that seems unstable. Ask yourself if you'll get tired of this particular thing in the next five years? Ask yourself if you would still be enjoying the same thing even if you weren't getting paid for it? This is how to find and know your passion. If your answers to the aforementioned questions are "yes," then you have found your passion. Find it by determining what you are exceptionally good at. Mine is writing, and I'd write even if I wasn't getting paid for it. Finding your niche will not only help you express yourself with passion, it will also reduce your odds of quitting. So, to start expressing yourself passionately, you need to find a topic you are passionate about.

Master the art of eloquence: The second step in expressing passionately is to master the art of eloquence. If you have read any book by Steve Harvey, or watched him on TV, then you know what it means to be eloquent. You can hear the eloquence and passion in his voice from a distance. To be eloquent is to attempt to insert your persuasive ideas into the mind of another person by using the art of language charm. Eloquence is the weapon of an influencer and any public speaker; when wielded properly, human minds will bow to your ideas. It is a way to get your message into the mind of your audience forever. What does that tell you? Eloquence is the best way to create an impression. True eloquence is emotionally powerful; it arouses the feelings of your audience. The human mind is sieve-like; it retains so little because we are easily distracted. However, eloquence helps you grab the atention of your audience by involving their emotions in what you are trying to say. It allows you to touch the chords of their hearts. Does this even make sense at all? Well, let's look at a real life example: For a class presentation some time ago in my college, our professor had chosen three different speakers to discuss a classic novel called *Wuthering Heights*. The first student was an incoherent speaker who kept going around in circles and beating around the bush, and you could see that she believed she was saying something interesting within herself. After five minutes of her wasting everyone's time, the professor booed her off the podium. The second speaker was more articulate; she talked about the novel and was audible, but her mode of communication was not persuasive enough. The third speaker was an eloquent speaker; she stole our attention with her impeccable usage and direct choices of words. She explained the plot of the story as though she were the real writer of the book; we could feel her passion for the characters in the story, and this made the whole class shower her with applause as soon as she rounded up her presentation. Even today, I still remember 80 percent of what she discussed that day. That's because she combined eloquence with simplicity to deliver a passionate speech. Well, I'm sure you don't want to be anything but an eloquent speaker and content writer as well. Eloquence is a skill that can be learned, practiced, and mastered.

Know your convictions: One important thing you need to know after learning eloquence is to know exactly what your take is on a particular topic. I have come to realize that those who are very good at making an impression are those who are not scared of expressing their views about a particular thing. You need to know if you are "for" or "against" a topic and let it show through your content. Your strong distaste or fondness about a thing or idea will show how passionate you are. Don't worry about people who may counter your opinions; you need to know that some people will not always be on your side and won't see things from your point of view; this is normal and also very good for an influencer because you need the engagement of your audience. In addition to firmly knowing your beliefs, you need to find and recognize your own voice to sound more authentic and passionate.

Tell real life stories: If you want your audience to be on the same page with you, you need to tell real life stories; let them be able to connect with you and relate to your content. You will find that the most impressive and inspiring content usually has something you can relate to and contains real life stories. Being genuine is one way to be passionate; remember, you can't fake it and make it in the social media world. Your audience can always tell when you are trying to be someone else. Passion can be expressed through real and inspiring stories.

Communicate in an entertaining manner: One way to be passionate with your expression is to make sure your content isn't boring. You don't need to be a standup comedian to express passionately, but humor is an essential communication tool. Making your audience laugh while passing on an important message keeps them relaxed and focused at the same time. We all love people with a sense of humor, and if you happen to be an amusing person, your audience will always look forward to hearing from you. One way to keep your audience interested and to not bore them is to make witty comments once in a while. Let's compare these two ads and see the power of humor. A boring and simple ad for a cologne will be something like this: "You really can't resist the charm of using the Creed cologne; you need to smell nice and make everyone fall in love with you. Choose CREED, any day anytime." Hmm, fair, you say. Now let's see the impact of humor and storytelling in advertising the same cologne. "Mr. Jones kept wondering why everyone always held their breath whenever he stepped into the office. His boss had also insinuated that he smelt like rotten egg one morning. Just like a guardian angel, Creed, the divine fragrance, landed in Mr. Jones's hands on Valentine's Day; it had come with the package his darling wife had sent him, and Mr. Jones just couldn't help the tears! He wept like a baby. Finally, he could have his friends back and smell nice once again. Everywhere Mr. Jones went, he held his head up high; everyone wanted to talk to him again, and just like an alcoholic, Mr. Jones would clutch a bottle of Creed in his arms everywhere he went. Get Creed now! It's your guardian angel." Obviously, the second advertisement would not be forgotten in a hurry. It only explains the power of wit and storytelling in expressing your passion.

Actionable steps to start expressing with passion

You have read how to be passionate in expressing yourself. Now, let's review the steps you'll need to take to start expressing yourself passionately. The first thing is to find your passion. Now how do you find your passion? You can find your passion by asking yourself these questions:

How do you spend your leisure time? What do you find yourself doing when you are free? This might give you a clue to determine what intrigues you.

What topics intrigue you? What kind of novels do you find appealing? What kind of programs do you look forward to seeing every time?

What clubs or magazines do you subscribe to?

Will you know your passion by asking yourself these questions? Let's see how I would answer the questions:

How do I spend my leisure time? I spend my time reading books on personal development and marketing.

What topics really intrigue me? Topics about marketing intrigue me, especially the ones that talk about meeting the needs of a target audience and advertising in an eye-catching manner.

What clubs or magazines do I subscribe to? I am a member of different online marketing groups, and I also enjoy reading and watching very intelligent and convincing ads.

Now what is my passion? My passion is MARKETING; I enjoy being a marketer and making really interesting ads. This is how to find your passion with these aforementioned questions.

The second tip to start expressing yourself passionately to get to work on your eloquence. How can you master the art of eloquence?

Start using vivid words that everyone understands in your daily conversations. Play on people's imagination by describing and painting a picture of what you are trying to say.

Make sure you are communicating by ensuring that your audience is listening to you. Pause to ask questions.

Use deliberate rhetoric techniques.

Make sure your content and ideas are convincing enough.

The third tip is to know your views; let your audience know if you are for or against an opinion, and be passionate about your opinion stating exactly why you do or don't support an idea.

· · ·

The fourth tip is the use of real-life stories. How can you do this?

Write down your ideas and try to determine if something similar has ever happened before.

You can research online to see if there are any real-life accounts that communicate your idea.

You can also ask family and friends if it has happened to them or someone they know.

The last tip is to use of wit and humor to make your content fun to read and entertaining. How can you do this?

Be unpredictable; go outside the lines to take your audience by surprise and write something they wouldn't expect within your content.

Use wit and comedy to liven up your content.

CHAPTER TWO: ENGAGING YOUR AUDIENCE

How do I keep my audience engaged as an influencer? How do I know exactly what my audience really wants, and how do I keep them interested in reading my content? We have all seen people whose number of followers do not match the engagement on their page. How can you have over two million followers, yet barely have up to one thousand likes or no more than one hundred comments on a post? This is really bizarre, and I'm certain no one wants to go through that. Now the golden question is: how do I get 90 percent of my audience interested and engaged with my content? This is quite simple, but it will require a lot of dedication and commitment to achieve.

HERE ARE THE TOP 15 TIPS TO HELP YOU GET YOUR AUDIENCE HOOKED ON YOUR CONTENT FOREVER.

BE CONSISTENT: The very first trick you need to learn as an influencer is CONSISTENCY. The sad news is you cannot be an influencer if you struggle with consistency; however, like every other skill, consistency can be learned, practiced, and mastered. Whether you are in the mood or not, you have to post constantly to attract your audience's interest and to keep them interested. Every successful influencer would tell you that this trick is the first one you need to learn, because everyone gets annoyed to have to wait for a very long time before hearing from people who influence or inspire them. So, how do I become consistent? I really want to post more often and be more active, but I just end up giving up somewhere along the line? How can I learn to be consistent until I have reached my goals? Just as mentioned earlier, consistency can be learned, practiced, and mastered. In order to be consistent in anything, you need to set short-term realistic goals; know exactly what you want to be consistent at and define it. Instead of saying, "I want to be consistent with my content," you should say, "I want to post every day and do online research one hour every day." This is more realistic and well defined. Set reminders where you can easily see them. If you make mistakes, do not give up. If you fail to live up to the goals you have set, this doesn't make you a failure; make sure you restart the following day if you fail to post yesterday; do not condemn yourself or consider yourself inconsistent. Remember, Rome wasn't built in a day; consistency is a gradual skill and cannot be mastered in a day. Being consistent doesn't mean you have to work at a stretch without taking a break; you need to take time off to relax and recharge. This simply means that in order to develop good content, you need to meditate often. Being consistent with zero productivity amounts to nothing. Make sure your aim is to create quality content while being consistent at the same time. Finally, after succeeding with your short-term goals, make sure you reward yourself.

POST QUALITY CONTENT: The second tip to get your audience's engagement is to post quality content on your platforms. Make sure you use smartphones with very good cameras to take your pictures or use a real camera; the majority of people are drawn to glamorous pictures. Also, make sure your pictures convey the ideas you want to pass across. We all get hooked on content with eye-catching and glamorous photos. Try using natural and bright light by turning off your phone's flash; the flash on your smartphone is still just a LED light that can give a strange hue to your photographs. Shooting with natural light sources helps make your pictures look more professional. You can also find a bright spot by a window if you are snapping indoors, but don't forget that certain shadows should be avoided by keeping light sources in front of you. If you prefer shooting outdoors, midmorning and late afternoon are typically the best time for optimal lighting for taking professional-looking photos. You can also use tripods to keep your smartphone or camera still. The major rationale behind all of this is to take clear pictures for your content in order to keep your audience engaged.

Add genuine and interesting captions: One other important thing you need to know about engaging your audience is to add genuine and interesting captions to your content. In order to keep people from scrolling past your content, you have to engage their minds and appeal to their intelligence. In order to do this, use the skill you learned in Chapter One: express with passion in order for your audience to feel and relate to your content. Show your audience that you are genuinely interested in the content you have created. Have you ever seen a very intelligent and interesting caption and wondered how the writers of such captions came up with them? Well, this is not difficult to do; all you need to do is to communicate intelligently with one of these three things:

Appeal to your audience's sense of humor: use humor to attack certain issues confronting your audience.

Ask really intelligent questions: when you throw intelligent questions at your audience, they will be forced to give you a reply and express their opinions. This will keep them engaged.

Tell real life stories and keep your captions real: in order to write really interesting captions, you can tell a story and keep your audience engaged with their desire to find out what happens in your story.

Use up to four relevant hashtags: As a social media influencer, another way to get people to notice your content more easily is to create up to four relevant hashtags; this will not only help people find your content, it can also improve engagement. If your content is about fashion, you have to use about four hashtags relating to fashion. An example of this is: #Fashion #Trendywear #femalewear #beautystyle. You can use any number of relevant hashtags depending on your content.

Follow back some of your followers: How would you feel if someone whose content inspires you so much or your favorite influencer follows you back? You would definitely feel great, right? You should try to follow back some of your followers whose accounts you enjoy as well and replying to comments left by your audience. Interacting with your audience also boosts their engagement. Try asking your audience to do certain things for a follow back. Perhaps ask them to comment their names without interruption for a follow back. Also, replying to their comments makes them want to comment more often, and that also boosts engagement on your content.

. . .

BE CHARISMATIC: There's no doubt indeed that charisma is one of the most captivating traits anyone can possess. It involves a lot of self-assurance to be charismatic. Being a charismatic influencer will not only draw people to you, it helps you create highly impressive content. First, you need to be really confident in order to become charismatic. People can sense the confidence lurking behind your content even without ever setting their eyes on you. To engage your audience, let your charisma show through your content. Let your audience see how sure you are about what you want to talk about. Don't worry about haters; they are everywhere. They are just very bitter people who are waiting for any opportunity to transfer their bitterness and make you feel bad. You will always come across these people no matter how charismatic and confident your content really is. The ironic truth about haters is that they are your biggest fans, obviously jealous of how successful you are becoming or the future prospect of excellence they see in you. Do not pay attention to such people while trying to engage your audience; instead, work on your self-confidence and set a daily reminder to tell yourself how wonderful an influencer you are going to be. Keep positive thoughts only and tell yourself what a good impact you will have on this world. Positivity spreads and people will embrace this positive vibe from you; they will look for your content anytime they need to stay positive.

BE AN EXPERT AT WHAT YOU DO:

The final and most productive step is to be really good at what you do. Being an influencer has to do with having meaningful content. In order to achieve this, you have to narrow your content in order to give your best. How do you narrow your content? If your content is about sports, in order to deliver your best, you should narrow it down to a particular specialty like swimming or running; your audience will know you are really good at what you do and can trust you more than if you are talking about everything under sports.

ACTIONABLE STEPS ON HOW TO ENGAGE YOUR AUDIENCE

ω Make sure you post regularly and be consistent with your content.

ω Attach quality pictures to your content in order to best convey your ideas.

ω Include about four or more relevant hashtags to your content as well as your location.

ω Reply to comments regularly and follow back some accounts you like.

ω Pick a feed planner app for your content. This will help you schedule posts.

ω Add genuine and interesting captions to engage your audience.

ω Use natural light for your photos.

CHAPTER THREE: HOW TO COLLABORATE WITH OTHER INFLUENCERS

It is essential to learn one of the major tricks of influencing—the trick of collaboration. In order to expand your follower base and reach out to more audiences, you can collaborate with another influencer who has a similar niche with you or who already has your target audience. Now what does this mean? It means that you cannot have everyone follow your brand all the time. Who is your target audience? If you feel that those who can benefit from your content are teenagers, you need to know who they are following right now and try to collaborate with such people; you will reach more of the people you want to and expand your target audience. In the influencing world, you should not be afraid to take chances and reach out to those who can help you grow. Now, how do you collaborate with other influencers and in what ways can you benefit from collaborating with other influencers?

You can brainstorm ideas together: You can collaborate with other influencers by thinking of wonderful ideas together that would be appealing to your audience. You can embark on a project together and let your audience know about such projects. When the both of you carry your audiences along with this project, it keeps them interested in your content. What am I saying here? You must have seen two or more of your favorite influencers come together on a venture, and it made you want to check the other person out and an perhaps follow them. You might have even seen some influencers of opposite sex who would pull a "dating stunt" just to make people follow or check the other person's brand out. Don't be surprised—it's a trick of collaboration. It works like magic. I personally know an influencer who specializes in creative writing; he writes books, poems, and short stories. He has a large follower base and has a lot of impact on his audience. When he wanted to reach more people, he collaborated with another influencer by writing a book with him. Not only did his follower base skyrocket, he also helped the other influencer become more popular. This is exactly how collaboration works in the influencing world.

Guest post on each other's platforms: Have you been thinking about collaborating with another influencer, but you are simply clueless on how to go about it? You can achieve this simply by guest posting on the other influencer's blog and have them do the same on yours. Don't be afraid to reach out; the worst they could say is *no*. A lot of them would be flattered that you want them to guest post on your platform. You would be sharing your audiences with each other by doing this; make sure the influencer is someone who has a similar niche with yours, and you are good to go.

CREATE VLOGS TOGETHER: Wouldn't you be intrigued if you saw your favorite influencers together in a video? I definitely would be intrigued. You can use this method to reach out to more audiences while making your more content fun as well. All you need to do is come together with an influencer you love and make a video together. Making a vlog with other influencers is one sure way to reach out to millennials. When you make videos together, it might just be a hangout or just something fun; you might be having an interesting discussion in the video which would sound appealing to your audience. Remember, you do not need to depart from your content. You only need to tag each other, and by so doing, you share your audiences with each other.

Take pictures with them and tag them: One other sure way to collaborate with other influencers is to take pictures and tag each other on your platforms. Remember the major reason behind collaborating with other influencers is to reach out to more people, so you have to ensure that the influencers you are collaborating have more, and not less, of a follower base than you. When you tag these influencers and they also tag you on their platforms, you both have access to more audiences.

Review the products and content of other influencers: One great way to get the attention of other influencers to collaborate with you is to review their content and products. If you like the content of a particular influencer or product, you might post a review on your own platform and tell your own audience what you really like about the content; your opinion will get them to notice you. When you reach out to such influencers later for a collaboration, it is easier for them to give in to your requests, because you have shown them you are a fan of their brand. Achieving a collaboration with people whose content you have reviewed automatically forges a connection between you and them.

. . .

COMING TOGETHER TO DO GIVEAWAYS: Everyone loves a giveaway; in fact, it is one of the greatest tools in getting the attention of your audience. Collaborating with other influencers to do giveaways will not only enable you reach out to a lot of people, it will also prompt people to recommend your platform to others as well. When influencers come together to fund giveaways, a lot of people are intrigued and compelled to check out the content and platforms of all the influencers involved.

USE SHOUT OUTS AS A COLLABORATION TECHNIQUE: Making a shout out on your platform and having other influencers do the same for you can boost your follower base. How do you make a shout out? You make a shout out by saying some nice things about other influencers on your platform and encouraging your audience to follow them or check them out. A lot of influencers have used this shout out technique to collaborate and get more followers. You can use it, too.

HOSTING PARTIES TOGETHER: Another way to collaborate with other influencers is to host parties together. When influencers host parties together, it helps create awareness for their brands. When you host or attend such parties, find every opportunity to promote your brand and make the most of it. Creating hashtags for the event, making posters for your brand, snapping quality photos, and making quality videos will also go a long way in helping you reach more of an audience.

HOW TO TAKE THE BOLD STEP TO REACH OUT TO OTHER INFLUENCERS?

Now you know how to use collaboration techniques to create more awareness. But how do you walk up to these influencers to let them know you want a collaboration with them? You really want to, but perhaps you just don't know how to make your intentions known to them. A lot of these influencers have built on their charisma and carved such a niche for themselves that they are confident and command a lot of respect. This makes some people conclude they are unapproachable or come off as snubs, but most times, this is not true at all; when you make your intentions of a collaboration known to them, a lot of them might be willing to help you, and you might even be surprised to know that some of them are really kindhearted and very approachable. Now how do you begin the journey of asking for a collaboration?

¬ Send them an email: a lot of busy people, especially influencers, take email very seriously. Just get their email address from their bio and send a professional message to them.

¬ Keep the note simple and professional: when reaching out to an influencer for a possible collaboration, make sure your message is simple, short, and straight to the point.

¬ Let them know you are a fan: if you are trying to reach an influencer for a collaboration, let them know that you love what they do, and you are a fan of theirs. This would help them really consider working with you.

Actionable steps on how to collaborate with other influencers.

Now that we have seen how powerful collaborating really is, you need to know exactly how to take the bold step of establishing a collaboration with that influencer of your choice today.

- The first step is to email them stating your intentions.

- The second step is to propose great ideas on what to do together.

- The third step is to meet with these influencers to communicate your ideas.

- The next step is to introduce each other on your platforms.

- Interview each other.

- Make videos and take photos together to post on your platforms.

- Make a shout out about each other on your platforms.

- Host parties together and invite your audience.

- Sponsor giveaways together.

CHAPTER FOUR: INSPIRING YOUR TRIBE

Get your audience to fall in love with you and your content.

Being an influencer has quite a lot to do with gaining the trust of your audience and making them fall in love with your content. If you want your audience to recommend your platform to other people and get totally hooked on your content, you have to create a bond to achieve this. You must be inspiring and impactful to achieve this. People who find it really easy to inspire people are lovable people; they know exactly how to reach the emotions of their audience and make themselves really irresistible. This means that they put the interests of other people first, and they make sure they carry others along by sharing their success stories and conquests. We all have role models—they are people who inspire us to become more. We look up to them even from a distance and find their personalities really intriguing. Sometimes we even love them to the extent that we stand up for them when people say bad things about them. This is because they INSPIRE us.

Now, let's see how you can inspire your tribe and make them fall head over heels in love with you. To inspire your tribe, you need to put the following things into consideration.

Be focused: This might sound really obvious, but a lot of people find it really difficult to be focused. How many times have you abandoned a project that seemed really interesting at first only to pick up another entirely different one? I remember how a lot of my peers would find a particular activity really intriguing at first only to abandon it for something new. This happens a lot of time; we tend to lose focus sometimes. It might just be a loss of interest or a loss of vision. This is why people have a lot of unfinished projects. Apparently, if you want to inspire your tribe, you have to concentrate on your defined goals and not digress from what you are known for. If you are a sports influencer, you have no business writing content about estate management. Your audience would probably be disappointed if you do this. You want to stay focused and consistent to be an inspiration to your audience. Let people know that you are an expert at what you do—you don't want to come off as a jack of all trades and master of none. Although you might be tempted to talk about things unrelated to what you are used to, if you feel you absolutely must pass the message across, make sure you apologize for straying and let your audience know you wouldn't be posting something unusual unless you thought it could be beneficial to them.

Staying authentic should be your goal: If you feel the need to inspire your tribe, you'll want to reach out to your audience's heart strings and gain their trust and complete loyalty. In order to do this, you have to stay genuine and be original. Let them see through you and know exactly who you are. You need to be completely honest to make your audience trust you and fall in love with your content. We all have people whose personality we are drawn towards. Now ask yourself if you would still look up to that person if he/she changed or tried to be someone else entirely? Certainly not; we fall in love with people's personalities when we know almost everything about them. Even when we learn their weaknesses, we do not stop loving them. This is because people love really genuine and authentic people. This is the kind of relationship you need to establish with your tribe. Now, how do we stay authentic? Your first step to being authentic is to embrace yourself, your values, and your beliefs. Do not compromise your standards in order to fit in or please a set of people. They are your standards; you have probably lived by them all your life; they should be valued by the people around you. For example, if you believe in the equality of human rights, you should treat people equally, too. This is how to be authentic. You can also work on your authenticity by leaving friends who do things you wouldn't do or things you consider unethical. For instance, if your friends smoke and you don't, or you consider it wrong for certain reasons, do not ever be compelled to compromise your standards to suit their egos or make them happy. In order to stay authentic, you also need to express your thoughts and feelings regardless of what other people think. You deserve to be heard; do not be afraid of speaking. Your tribe will get inspired if you always do this. People develop a sense of admiration towards confident people. Everyone loves assertive people, and this would make you stand out and unique. One other way to be authentic is to share personal information about yourself and let your audience relate with you.

Offer assistance: If you think the main reason behind influencing is to get a large follower base and force your opinion down people's throat, then you are totally wrong. If you want your tribe to be inspired by your content, you need to make sure you are adding something to their lives and making them feel valued and appreciated for being a part of your brand. One excellent way to do this is to offer a helping hand to your audience. You could ask widows or orphans to identify themselves, and you can assist them in your own little way. You do not have to go beyond your limits; you should do what you can do within your capacity, and this would make you win the heart of your tribe and make them love you and have a deep sense of respect for you.

Do a meet and greet with your audience: If you want to connect with your tribe or audience on a more individual level, you should try to let them meet you in person to create personal relationships. Doing a meet and greet will not only help your audience feel like an important part of your brand, it makes them consider you as a friend afterwards. This is exactly what you need to maintain a friendly relationship with your tribe. Doing a meet and greet will work in your favor; establishing personal relationships with your audience helps inspire your audience.

Host live chats: In order to inspire your tribe, you need to develop a connection with them just as stated in the above bullet. One easy way to do this is to host live chats and answer questions they may have and relate to them through the use of humor, the sharing of ideas, and simply flowing along with your audience.

Help to advertise some of your audience's business: Helping to advertise your followers' businesses on your platform for free is also a great and thoughtful way to inspire your audience. This would mean so much to them and make them love you and respect you more, because it shows you really value them and their interests by taking the time out to advertise their business for free. You should do this once in a while as it's a great way to give back to your audience.

Tell your story: One great way to inspire your tribe is to share your story with them. Tell them about things that could inspire them. Do not bore your audience by telling unnecessary stories; we do not need to know how you grew your first tooth. Only tell them things you feel they should know. Let your audience feel like they know you already. Do not hide things from them: if you are married, do not paint an image of being a single person. It would break the hearts of your audience if they found out otherwise. These little details count. To influence people is to have a place in their hearts; to impact people is to touch the chords of their hearts and create a shadow of yourself in their lives. To pass a message across to your audience, you must get their attention. One great way to grab the attention of your audience is to tell your story. Your story could be the key that unlocks someone else's prison—do not be afraid to share it.

Carry your audience along through a challenge: If you take up a challenge and carry your audience along, you inspire them by making them watch how you commenced the challenge and let them see you through the finish line as well. What does this mean? It means you could take up a weight loss challenge and make your intention known to your audience. Carry them along by showing them videos of your workouts and all. Tell them how it feels like, and show them how you do it; by the time you get your desired result and tell your audience, they feel genuinely happy because they were a part of the challenge and may feel inspired to do the same as well. It does not necessarily have to be a weight loss challenge; there are several other types of challenges you could take up.

Be accommodating: When your audience seeks you out to get your advice, you should try not to be a snub as this could cause you to lose your followers and lose their love and trust. You need to lend a listening ear to them and pay attention to their interests, giving advice when necessary, and empathizing with them when necessary. To be accommodating means you have to sacrifice your time to pay attention to the needs of other people and put them first. Learning how to accommodate people helps to inspire them and build their trust. In order to make your tribe one group of happy and satisfied people, you need to reach out and be accommodating to your audience.

Stay emotionally strong: You might want to ask how staying emotionally strong will help you inspire people, or the connection between the two, but there is indeed a connection. To serve as an inspiration to people, you need to first work on your own emotional stability. This shows through the way you handle trolls. If you have a habit of always bashing people who troll you, it might have a negative effect on your audience as this could portray you as a weakling and as someone who is emotionally unstable. To inspire people means you want to preach a message, and to do this, you need to live by example. When people troll you or say negative things about you, you need to use the power of silence; it doesn't make you stupid, it only makes you appear mature, and that will earn you a deep respect from your audience. You could even reply to some people with nice comments; people would notice this and respect you for it. Remember, it's social influencing; some naysayers would definitely take pride in watching you quit, but to reach your goals faster, you need to ignore all distractions and concentrate on your well-defined goals.

Educate your audience: Educating your audience doesn't mean you have to get a blackboard and chalk; it means that there ought to be a message behind all content. Before posting on your platforms, ask yourself what your audience stands to gain from your content. You need to ensure every post is beneficial. If you find something helpful or something that could help your audience in a certain way, don't be stingy; share it with your audience. Drop links to certain helpful posts that could educate your audience. Share your latest findings with them, and make sure there's something to learn from every post. When educating your audience, do not force people to like you or be inspired; just keep it really simple and natural.

ACTIONABLE STEPS ON HOW TO INSPIRE YOUR TRIBE.

After reading this chapter, you will feel really passionate and ready to inspire your tribe or audience. In order to set the ball rolling, here are the steps you need to take.

» Be authentic by letting your audience see through you. Do not try to be someone else. Keep your content very honest.

» Let your audience get to know you on a more personal level by telling your story and having a meet and greet once in a while or hosting live chats with them.

» Be genuinely interested in your audience by relating with them well, advertising their platforms sometimes, and giving them advice when they reach out to you.

» Educate your audience by sharing new things with them and making every post meaningful.

» Inspire your audience by taking up a challenge and carrying them along through the whole process.

» Cultivate an inspiring attitude by genuinely caring for people and being accommodating.

CHAPTER FIVE: ATTRACTING THE IDEAL AUDIENCE:

now how to reach out to the people who vibe with your content.

One of the key factors about communicating with a whole lot of people is finding and attracting your ideal audience. Being an influencer means reaching out to the members of the public, but your content might not be for the consumption of the general public. You need to know how to reach out to the correct audience. The following techniques will help you attract the right following and get the people who can vibe along with your content.

KNOW YOUR TARGET AUDIENCE: The very first thing you need to understand about attracting the ideal audience is to first define who your audience is. Once you know this, attracting them is a lot easier than you think. You have probably heard the saying "Know your audience" over a dozen times already, so now let's analyze what this really means and how helpful this can be to an influencer. You already know the meaning of an audience: they are the people who are expected to read and benefit from your content. Just as it is almost impossible for a ten-year-old to be interested in topics like "aging and how to cope with its challenges" and how totally ridiculous it would be for a thirteen-year-old boy to be interested in "diaper changing and post-natal care," certain topics are meant for a certain audiences. Knowing the people you want to communicate with helps you understand, determine, and implement the right tactics and terminologies while communicating. After you have decided on the kind of audience you want to establish a communication or connection with through your content, you need to know if you have been getting attention from your target so far and what type of audience your content really attracts. One way to do this is to track your content traffic with Google Analytics. Google Analytics will help you find out who visits your site and how they are getting there. You want to know exactly the kind of people your content attracts and how they learned about you. Well, Google Analytics helps you to stop guessing and be exactly sure of the kind of people who have been interested in your content thus far. You can learn the exact ages of such people: if most who frequent your site are below 40 and above 25, this helps you understand that your target audience so far has been people between the age of 26-39. Google Analytics also shows you the countries of the people visiting your content. You can learn if a majority of those who frequent your site are Americans, Asians, or Africans. Google Analytics also tells you exactly how these people get to your site and the option that works best for you among the most common options, namely via direct, organic, referral, social, paid, or email. All these are shown by Google Analytics. It can also show you what kind of devices your audience is using and if you should make your content available for all three: mobile, tablet, or desktop. All this information helps you to know if you are attracting the right audience and what to do to make amends. If you are curious about how to use Google Analytics, do not worry; you will be taught everything you need to know about tracking your traffic with Google Analytics. Keep your fingers crossed and keep reading. You might want to know if Google Analytics work for apps like Facebook, Instagram, or LinkedIn, and the answer is *Yes*. If you have been using Instagram or Facebook for your influencing career, you need not worry, because Google Analytics can help you track your audience on these apps.

HOW DO I USE GOOGLE ANALYTICS?

If you have been thinking about using Google Analytics to find your audience, this is how to go about it:

• Go to google.com/Analytics

• Create an account and click Start for Free

• Set up a property (your website or app) in your analytics account

• Set up a reporting view in your property

• Follow the instructions to add the tracking code to your website or mobile app, so you can collect data in your analytics property.

Now you can set the ball rolling and find your audience. Know exactly who your audience is, their countries, and the kind of device they use.

• • •

Create the right content: After knowing who your audience is, the next step to attracting the ideal audience is knowing exactly the right content your audience would be interested in. You need to know the problems confronting your audience and ensure your content provides enough answers to such problems. When creating content, you should ask yourself these questions: Does my content solve any problem my audience may have, and what do they stand to gain from this content? How different is my content from that of my competitors? You need to ensure your content is about your audience and not you. Redirecting the attention from yourself to them makes your content worth reading. This gives your audience the feeling that you hold their interests dear to your heart. You also need to ensure that your content doesn't go out of context. In order to create the right content, you should first brainstorm the ideas you really want to convey and write them down. Make sure to extensively research your ideas in order to provide complete information; you do not want to come off as having a low IQ when your audience asks questions not included in your content. Make sure your content is written in a very conversational and easy to read manner; do not include jargon, deep words, and unnecessary adjectives. You must ensure your content is very easy to understand by making your audience feel really comfortable while reading; ensure it is as straightforward as possible. You also need to know what kind of content drives traffic on your site or blog. It is essential to elaborate, but you have to ensure every paragraph drives home your point. Ensure that the whole content is not boring and conservative. You can also determine which content has the highest views through Google Analytics. It helps you see the content with the highest page views and know what is being shared as well. When Google Analytics helps you determine this, you know exactly what your audience is interested in and you can learn and apply the same techniques to new content.

. . .

Offer unique features: In order to attract the ideal audience, you need to ensure that you have something different to offer your readers. Check what others are doing. Know what your competitors are doing and do yours differently. Doing a different thing doesn't mean you have to change your focus, it only means that you need to be creative. Creativity has never been useless and applying it to your content as an influencer will make you stand out and be different. Set new rules and do not be afraid of a little alteration and inventiveness—it's not bad to try. When you apply creativity to your content, it gives your audience the message that says "Choose me even though there are millions of others out there." One major way to create unique content is to take a stand. I know this has been mentioned often in this book, but in order to take a leap and attract the ideal audience, you need to oppose the majority opinion if you feel you should. If other influencers promote things you would not promote or you feel otherwise about, you should never try to sideline your own opinions. You want an ideal audience, and this would go a long way in helping you to attract them. Your own real audience will vibe along with your content and see things from your perspective. One way to offer unique content is not just about writing that perfect, mind-blowing idea in your journal; it will simply stay in your head or in your journal if you do not act on it. I know a friend who had this very awesome idea and shared it with me. It was his own innovation. The idea was a very lovely one, but he didn't put it to work on time. The following week, someone had come up with an almost identical idea, and my friend just couldn't believe it. He kept swearing to himself that the idea had been totally his, and he was really disappointed. Now what happened to my friend's idea? In case you were wondering if someone snitched his wonderful idea, then you are wrong. The truth is that everyone is working and thinking of how to improve and do something different, so if you develop a wonderful idea, you had better not sleep on it. Put it to work immediately, because someone else from a totally different country and climate might outwit you and put it out before you do.

Never imagine your audience is like you: Although it is really nice to be original while creating your content, a lot of influencers make the mistake of always assuming their audience will always reason like them. Do not forget that influencing has a lot to do with making an impact in the lives of people, and it's a global world we live in today where you reach people of different races, colors, religions, and political views. It would be very wrong to assume everyone is black or white, or everyone likes the same color you like. Creating content for a global audience means you have to consider the differences in terminology. These differences exist even between cities. What do we mean by this? In the US, what is known as a "potato chip" is called "crisp" in the UK. Once you already know the countries your audience are coming from through Google Analytics, it would be much easier to identify these differences. You should never make your content ambiguous if you want to reach your ideal audience. To avoid ambiguity, you should learn to keep your sentences short and avoid the use of double negatives. Do not use abbreviations. When you do this, you assume your audience already knows the meaning, and you may lose the attention of your audience as they might stop reading to look up the full meaning of the abbreviated words. If you must use abbreviations like SME, you should write the full meaning in front of the short form, and not assume that everyone knows the meaning is "subject matter expert." Getting rid of this assumption helps you clearly communicate so even a layman will understand your message. When you do not assume that everyone shares your religious beliefs or skin color, you make it easier to attract your ideal audience across the globe as well.

. . .

Make the problems your content solves really obvious: I'm sure nobody would be interested in reading content that doesn't have a particular goal. When we stumble upon a page, a website, or post, the very first thing that comes to the mind is "what exactly is this content all about?" You want to know if the content deals with fashion, sports, business, or travel. After checking out five posts or more and the main point behind the content is still not clear, you might lose interest. This is a turn off for your audience, and I'm sure you don't want to put your audience through that. However, when you find yourself scrolling through a blog or page that tells you all you need to know about the page after reading just one post, and the entire content screams the reason behind its existence, you instantly want to follow, read more, and subscribe if it's exactly what you need. The logic behind it is quite simple: it's like having to choose between a boutique with tinted windows that has no billboard or signage outside to tell you that clothing is being sold inside or a boutique that has well-dressed mannequins showing through vivid windows with large and colorful signs that say, "WE SELL CLOTHES." A sane person would definitely go for the latter, because a lot of people won't be able to assume what you do; they want to know for sure and you have to do the telling. Let it show through your bio that this is exactly what you do. Your ideal audience wants a solution to their problem, and your job is to let them know you are the person they can trust. Have you ever come across content that gave you exactly what you wanted or appeared really intriguing, and you just hissed and scrolled through nonchalantly? This doesn't seem to be what a normal person would do. When you find something really intriguing, whatever it is just crawls up into your heart and rents an apartment in there for as long as you still find that particular thing intriguing. You would never hiss or scroll through indifferently; you would definitely stop to read more intriguing things from the same person. This is exactly the first impression you want your ideal audience to have about you. In order to follow this attraction principle, you need to make the problem your content solves really obvious.

COMPILE QUESTIONS YOUR AUDIENCE REALLY WANT ANSWERS TO: Zig Ziglar once said, "You will get what you want in life if you help other people get what they want." This simply means that if you really want to engage your ideal audience, you need to stop assuming you know the questions on their mind. Tell them you can help them, and you will get the audience you really need. You need to make the interests of your audience your priority if you want them to vibe along with your content. How do you do this? Connect with your audience on a more personal level in order to get to the questions on their mind. Once you have these real-life questions from your target audience, the next thing is to compile these questions and provide answers to them. One thing that has also helped a lot of influencers boost their relationship with their audience is asking for a feedback. When you reach out to your audience and ask them questions on what you could do to deliver better content to them, it not only shows you what your audience thinks about your content, it also boosts your relationship with them. It makes them feel really valued and important to your brand. This will definitely help you attract your ideal audience.

ACTIONABLE STEPS ON HOW TO ATTRACT YOUR IDEAL AUDIENCE

Now that you know how important it is to reach your ideal audience, you must be ready to set the ball rolling to find and attract them. The following steps are the summary of the high-lighted ways to attract your perfect audience:

• The very first step is to set up a Google Analytics account, which helps you track the traffic on your content and learn who is attracted to your content.

• The second step is to create a good content. You should ensure your content is easily understood and problem solving. You should avoid the use of abbreviations and jargons as well as ambiguity in your write-up.

• The third step is to offer unique features and apply creativity in order to stand out.

• The fourth step is to eradicate assumptions. Do not assume your audience knows everything you want to talk about already. You should try to educate and give thorough explanations.

• The fifth step is to ensure that everyone (including newbies) understands the message behind your content. Let the problems you solve show through your content. Include the things you do in your bio, so your audience will know if it's what they want, and they will choose to stay if they are interested in the services you provide.

• The last step is to boldly consult your audience for feedback on what they want to know more about and how they think you could improve the quality of your services.

Adhering to these rules will go a long way in helping you attract your ideal audience.

CHAPTER SIX: GET YOUR FIRST ONE THOUSAND TRUE FANS

The previous chapter explains in depth how to get your ideal audience, but in this chapter, you will be learning how to get your first one thousand true fans. You might want to ask if there is a difference between an "ideal audience" and "true fans." This is a really interesting and intelligent question, but don't be surprised that there is indeed a huge difference between the two. Your ideal audience simply means your prospective audience, potential buyers, and the right people for your brand. However, when we talk about "true fans," they are the people who would root for your brand any day, anytime; they are the people who would recommend you to their friends or tell someone they have just met about you and your brand. Everyone around them knows they are in love with your product, your content and your brand. Have you ever asked yourself why people would leave their own country for a different country just to watch their favorite football team play or travel long distances to attend the concerts of musicians they love so much? These people are passion-driven; they are in love with these people and what they represent and are always rooting for them. Is there someone whose personality, product, or brand you love so much, and no matter how other people dislike them, you never stop loving them? Of course, we all have at least one such person in our lives; we just love them even though we may not have ever met them in real life. We call these people who have immense loyalty in your brand, content, and product, your true fans, and all you need to do right now is to imagine having a thousand of such people in your life. Do not aim too high for now; these one thousand true fans would buy whatever you sell to them, take your recommendations seriously, and never joke with your endorsements because they have a profound, genuine loyalty and trust in your brand. A lot of brands like Apple and Nike are a typical example of this. The customers of Apple would instantly buy a newly produced iPhone or any other product no matter how expensive. This is because of what Apple represents; every prospective buyer of theirs wants to be identified with what Apple represents. Why do you think a lot of people showoff the Apple logo? It is because they secretly desire to be identified with this brand that has carved a niche and reputation for itself. This is what everyone who wants to be identified with a brand says to themselves whether they realize it or not. Sometimes, it is not the brand itself but what the brand represents. To some people, an iPhone from Apple represents class; to some, it's just an identity; to some people, it is a trend they need to keep up with, while to others, it is an essential device. No matter the reason behind it, one thing is obvious, these people are all fans of the Apple brand and would buy whatever product this company puts out there.

The golden question, however, is how do I get these thousands of social media users to become my fans and get them identified with my brand? Well, that is why this book was conceived —to answer every question you have. With the following advice and recommendations, you will get your first one thousand true fans out of your ideal audience.

HOW DO YOU MAKE "TRUE FANS" OUT OF YOUR IDEAL AUDIENCE?

CARVE AN IDENTITY FOR YOUR BRAND: This is obviously a glaringly obvious step. Anyone who wants people to be identified with their brand must first have an identity themselves. Having an identity for your brand or content goes beyond having logos, trademarks, and a brand name. This simply means that you have to recognize your own voice as a brand, and let this voice resonate through your audience. You should be able to create an identity in such a way that even when other people plagiarize your content, your audience would bet it originally belongs to you. Of course, having a trademark brand name is part of it as well as a unique and eye-catching logo. However, the major thing about having an identity is to have your own style that stands out and distinguishes you among other influencers. This is what most writers, show hosts, and a lot of public figures do. A fan of Nora Roberts should be able to recognize her writing even when reading a book without a title. This is because these writers adopt a style of writing which is easily noticed by their readers. The same thing applies to every successful brand: having a voice as a brand advertises your product, showcases you to the public, and resonates this voice with members of the public. A brand that has no identity will find it really difficult to make huge waves and be known out there. In order to get your first one thousand true fans, you need to identify your own style and stand out as a brand.

SELL HOPE: One great way to get your first one thousand true fans is to sell hope through your content. Everyone wants to be reminded that awkward situations and not so great things can turn around for the better. So, one great way to reach out to the chords of the hearts of your audience is to sell hope to them. This is used in a tongue-in-cheek manner, and by selling hope, I do not mean opening a store where you sell hope to your audience literally. What do I mean by selling hope? Whatever thing you do, regardless of the area you influence, you can tell the story of hope to your audience. If you are a fashion influencer, you should sell hope to your ideal audience by letting them know that all hope is not lost for them, and you are there to help rejuvenate their fashion life. Let them know that no matter how many fashion blunders they might have made in life, you are there to help them make amends and you can make wonderful fashion icons out of someone who used to have zero fashion sense. Do not just say it, act it, preach the message of hope, and you will instantly gain true fans who would be ready to stick with you, your brand, your content, and what it represents for a very long time. If you are a fitness influencer, sell hope to your audience, help them regain their lost confidence by telling them they can get to their desired weight and help them achieve just want they want. In a society where people are constantly made to feel less important, where mediocrity is not applauded, and someone who is making an effort is told not to try, the least you can do is preach positivity. Doing this helps create a better place for your audience, and they will respond by reciprocating your kindness with love and utmost loyalty. Whatever you do, do not fail to tell people to never give up. When society wants them to bend over backwards, be the voice that constantly reminds them "they are enough and can be anything they set their minds to be." This might not sound like a professional theory or technique to you, but it is a tested and trusted one indeed. When people see that your content preaches hope and positivity, they instantly want to become identified with your brand and also recommend your content to someone else, because they also want to spread positivity and are proud of what your content represents.

PROMOTE YOUR CONTENT: In order to get your very first one thousand true fans, you should try as much as possible to introduce your brand to new and totally different people. I'm sure you must know by now that you should never think of buying followers. In case you missed that, do not ever try to buy followers. It's just so shady, and a lot of people can instantly tell when you do so, because the numbers just never add up. Instead of buying followers, you could use paid ads to boost your page and make your brand known to the members of the public. You could also feature your content in popular magazines and also ask your friends and family to recommend you. These are great ways to boost and promote your content in order to reach your true fans.

NURTURE EVERY RELATIONSHIP: One amazing way to reach your first one thousand fans is to nurture every new relationship you get with your audience. When new people reach out to you personally, you should pay attention to them and hear them out. You could use automated messages to reach out to new people who check out your content; it could just be a short welcome message or a "Thank you for checking out our page, and we look forward to working with you" kind of message; it doesn't need to be unnecessarily lengthy and boring. Everybody who has taken time out to check out your brand is really important to you and the growth of your brand as a whole; therefore, you need to nurture every relationship with your ideal audience by taking time out to pay them atten-tion as well. This is how to make true fans out of your ideal audience.

PRODUCE GREAT VALUE: It is a fact that nobody wants to be identified with a brand that swindles people for a living or a brand which provides very poor output. In order to get your first one thousand true fans, you should consider your reputation first. Like I said earlier, your fans are those ideal, prospective buyers of your content who would recommend your brand or content to the people they know. How do you expect people to recommend you if you do not produce great value or quality content? True fans are not interested in quantity; they are interested in what you have to offer. How quality is your service? Aside from the fact that having quality content helps you stand out from others, it gives your audience the impression that you are very much interested in making them happy and not just interested in what they have to offer. Producing great value and quality services would help you earn a name for your brand and also help you get your true fans.

LISTEN AND OBSERVE: Paying attention to the needs of your audience should be a priority if you really want to get your first one thousand true fans. This is simply because there are several other people out there who are doing the same thing as you, and your audience would be quick to identify with you if you do not take their love for granted. You must have heard that having your first one thousand true fans has a lot to do with having a long email address list; of course, this is not a fallacy. In order to have this long list of emails, you have to listen to your audience, and observe what they really want. Know when they do not buy the idea you are presenting and be brave enough to ask them why they do not believe in your idea. Only a brave person would be ready to admit his mistakes and ask for the opinions of other people. There will definitely be a time when you do not agree with the opinions of your audience. However, you do not need to be rude about it; say it in the nicest manner and back your opinions with tangible reasons.

BE DEDICATED: Dedication toward what you do helps people to understand how important your work is to you and how well you cherish what you do. In order to get people to fall in love with your brand, you have to be really committed and hard working. Be genuinely interested in what you do; do not get tired of reading and meeting new people to expand your knowledge. You don't need to be an expert at everything in life, but you have to be an expert when it comes to your brand; dedicating a lot of time to your content as an influencer would definitely help you get your first one thousand true fans, because they see how dedicated and committed you are, and they want to be identified with your brand.

ACTIONABLE STEPS ON HOW TO GET YOUR FIRST ONE THOUSAND TRUE FANS

• You need to first create an identity for your brand; your logo, trademark, and theme should be quite impressive. You should also try to identify your own voice and have this voice registered with your audience.

• After creating an identity for your brand, you should sell hope to your audience by teaching them to never give up on themselves and by making them trust your brand if they crave effective change in their lives.

• You should promote your content, not by buying followers, but by using paid ads, getting your content featured in popular magazines and asking for recommendations from family and friends.

• You should use automated messages to reply to people who might be checking out your content or reaching out to you for the first time. Let your audience know how important and special they are.

• You need to ensure that you deliver and produce a quality service to your audience.

• Paying attention to your audience by listening and observing will also help you get your first one thousand true fans faster.

• The last thing you need to do is remain dedicated and committed to what you do as everyone likes to be identified with a consistent brand.

CHAPTER SEVEN: TWELVE CONFIDENCE TECHNIQUES YOU NEED TO LEARN

*T*welve confidence techniques you need to learn in order to kick off as a successful influencer.

One thing everyone needs to know is that being confident will help you in every area of your life. Sometimes, a lot of people grow up hating a particular part of their body or even grow up wishing they did something differently. Do you look in the mirror and just end up wishing you had the face and body of a super model? Or sometimes you just feel like you are not good enough to succeed at what you do, or you just doubt your own talents and abilities? Whether your own lack of confidence stems from not having your desired body or you are just simply insecure about your career, the story doesn't change. Lack of confidence can definitely deprive you of so many things. The opposite of confidence is fear, self-doubt, and general insecurity. The moment your confidence begins to slip away, fear is welcomed into your heart, and you just give "self-doubt" an invite into your beautiful life. When fear gets a room in your heart, you become really scared of taking action that could be productive, and you also begin to doubt your own worth and start telling yourself you are not good enough. This is when you start producing results which are below your usual standards. In this chapter, you will learn how to produce quality content while being confident. When confident people gain entry into a gathering, their poise, looks, and actions pulls your attention towards them and makes them even more enigmatic. They look so unbothered, like they have no problems whatsoever in life. When you start a conversation with them, you just get hooked, and with a few sweet words, they have already melted your heart, and you just can't help but like them. These people often have a positive outlook towards life and a way of spreading positivity. They do not stutter when they talk, they have a good sense of humor, and often have a stand in life. They do not compare themselves with others and only try to be the best versions of themselves. Forbes once reported that a lot of successful people have only come that far because of their confidence. These confident people are not afraid of criticism and know exactly how to handle it. This ability to not give up regardless of what people say is "confidence" and has driven many to success. You can become successful, too, if you believe in confidence today.

The previous chapters in this book were more focused on how to improve your relationship with your audience. However, this particular chapter will be more focused on you and how to improve yourself and your confidence level. To influence people, you need to first work on yourself and become a good example. Being confident will definitely help you command respect and feel good as a person without underrating your own abilities, while also helping you become successful in your career.

· · ·

The following techniques will help you become more confident:

WORK TOWARD YOUR GOALS EVERYDAY: Working toward your goals everyday will definitely help you become proud of yourself. You might want to ask, "How do I work towards my goals?" Well, it's not easy, but you will be able to do this through determination. Once you are determined to achieve a goal, the vision becomes clearer, and every day becomes a step closer to your dreams. For example, your dream might be to reach a fan base of one million people or even more. Well, it's not bad to dream, but having a vision without working hard to achieve it only leaves your dream a fantasy, but working hard toward it makes it a reality. If reaching a fan base of one million people is your goal, you need to work towards your goal everyday by increasing your consistency and never losing your focus. Having a dream and working towards your goals will definitely help you become more confident.

NEVER STOP LEARNING: If you want to become really confident, you should embrace learning and never relent on doing just that. To become a confident person means to be sure; a lot of people feel that confident people are really knowledgeable. This is because they appear to know a whole lot even when they are not well knowledgeable in all areas. This simply means that you do not need to aim to be the best at everything, you only need to be best at what you do, because the bitter truth is, you can never know everything about the world, but you should try to at least know something about almost everything. If you desire to increase your knowledge, then you have to be very open to a wide range of information. Learn and never stop learning. Note that you are not learning to prove that you are way better than everyone, but only learning in order to boost your confidence and have a positive outlook about yourself. Being confident will help you develop the ideal attitude towards life. Have you also heard that confidence acts as a magnetic pull when it comes to attracting your ideal audience? Readers are leaders, and one great way to stay confident is to never give up on learning.

MAKE SURE YOUR VISION IS CLEAR: If you ever feel like you do not know what direction your career is headed in at any time, or you feel like you are just not doing something right, do not give up or ever feel incompetent or less of a person. There is a therapy that has helped a lot of entrepreneurs pull out of this phase; you only need to keep your eye on the bigger picture. Make sure your vision is really clear, and this way, you will never doubt your own standards or abilities. In this way, your confidence is boosted and rebuilt, and you will feel more sure, more certain even though you are still very far from your dreams. This will help you say levelheaded, more confident, and also help you become successful as an influencer.

SAY NO TO NEGATIVITY: Sometimes you read comments from people you have never met in your life. You instantly check to see if you know this person who is hating on you so much only to find out they live in an entirely different country. At that moment, you want to ask, "Why do you hate me so much? What have I done to deserve such hateful comments?" but at this moment, you should remember the popular saying that, "People are only allowed to hurt you with your own permission." Apparently, you are the only one who has the right to decide if you want to be hurt by a total stranger or not. I know you want to ask, "'What if this negativity was coming from someone from your inner circle?" Well, the answer to this is really obvious. When you have people from your own inner circle who derive joy in making you feel less of a person or feel like you aren't doing something right, well, I'm not sorry to say it's high time you bid them farewell. Say goodbye to them without ever looking back at them, because they do not deserve to be in your life. Anyone who wants to sabotage your career with hateful comments deserves to watch you succeed from a distance. Of course, it's nice to have constructive criticism once in a while, but you need to know the difference between advice and unsolicited, hateful comments. This is definitely one great way to remain confident and never doubt your own self-worth and abilities. The very moment someone says something hateful, be nice enough to pay them no attention. You will be doing yourself a lot of good, because a lot of people who go about hating on other people are simply jealous of them and bitter about their own situations. Do not get yourself worked up over someone else's disapproval. Other times, your mind may be the one giving room for negativity. When this happens, stop it, because you are exactly what you feed your mind. When the negative thoughts come, you should send them back to wherever they came from, and tell yourself positive things alone, read positive things, keep positive friends, and say only positive things. Your daily slogan should be, "Dear *wonderful self, you are capable of succeeding at anything you set your mind at.*" You are your number one fan and your own hype man; every change begins with you and you alone. When you allow positivity, it will radiate to everyone else around you.

DO NOT BE SCARED OF MAKING MISTAKES: Everyone battles with the fear of making mistakes. Even the most confident people do this once in a while. Hellen Keller once said, "Life is either nothing at all or some adventure." Life is actually nothing without risks. How do you learn to walk and stand firmly if you have never fallen before? When we fail in life, it teaches you the importance of success and makes you learn from your mistakes. How do you become confident with the fear of making mistakes still deeply rooted in your heart? Real confidence is when you are not scared of making mistakes but embracing the attitude that says, "no matter what cards I'm dealt or how many mistakes I make, I was built to be successful." Nurturing this thought will help you have an entirely different perspective towards life and help you to not lose your confidence or doubt your self-worth. A lot of great people have made mistakes, but the good news is they became successful because they didn't stop trying. Thomas Edison learned the one thousand ways that a light bulb won't work, because he failed one thousand times. The fact that you failed at something doesn't make you a failure, and the ability to keep this in mind will help you become really confident and successful in life.

DO NOT EVER MAKE ROOM FOR DOUBTS: How many times have you developed cold feet after being really sure about doing something in life? Sometimes we think we've got our life all figured out until we meet people who seem really skilled at the same thing we do. They seem better than you, and you just lose it all at that moment: your security and your confidence, and you let self-doubt take over. It is a fact that no matter how skilled or talented you are, you will always come across people who are better. No matter how good-looking you are, there's always someone who is better looking. This is not to say that you are not good at what you do, too, it's just that you have to understand the fact that there will always be other people, and when someone better than you comes around, you do not need to feel inferior; just be yourself and remind yourself of your own achievements. Remember how many wonderful comments you have received about your brand, and raise your head up high, and aim to be better than the person you were the previous day without room for doubt. Questions like, "Am I capable? Can I ever succeed with my career? Is this what I should be doing?" should never be allowed in your heart, because you ought to remind yourself of how wonderful you are at what you do, and how this world needs you to survive. Keeping this in mind will help you become a confident and successful person.

CELEBRATE LITTLE ACHIEVEMENTS: You can become really successful by celebrating little achievements. Should we celebrate little achievements? Does it even make sense to celebrate your 2k followers when others are looking for ways to attract more followers after reaching over 20 million followers? Well, this is exactly where confidence comes in; what sets you apart from people who do not still feel gratified after several millions of followers is gratitude. It might not sound logical to celebrate your ability to stay away from your cell-phone or chocolate a whole day, but you are the only one who knows how much these little things mean to you. Celebrating little achievements simply makes you more grateful, and it also increases your faith in your own abilities. It makes you under-stand that if you were actually able to succeed with little things, then your success with greater things should be guaranteed. It is possible to find people who are really successful but lack confidence. This is because they believe they were just lucky; they do not believe in their own abilities, and such people may end up not being successful for a long time. To become successful and confident, you need to own your success and have faith in your own capabilities. This can only happen when you do not forget to celebrate little achievements. The next time you meet a target, no matter how small, you could reward yourself with something really nice. It reminds you of how capable you really are and helps you become more confident.

. . .

GET ADVICE FROM YOUR ROLE MODELS: Everyone has someone they look up to as a mentor. These are people who are already where you aspire to be. They are people you respect for reasons known only to you and especially because they are successful doing what you want to do as well. You should get advice from such people and ask them to tell you about things you might possibly face in the long run. These people are already walking in the shoes you want to walk in; you might as well ask them how comfortable they are in the shoes, and why they have come so far, so that you do not trip in those same shoes when your time comes. A lot of role models would be eager to educate you and advise you. When you have the backing of your role models or when they commend your work, it boosts your confidence and makes you sure you are not doing something wrong. Their advice also keeps you on track and assists you in making the right decisions.

KEEP A LIST OF YOUR ACHIEVEMENTS: Keeping a list of your achievements in a journal makes your progress accessible to you when you tend to lose faith and become uncertain about your own self-worth. Reviewing achievements has helped a lot of people stay confident. You can try it as well. It also helps you stay focused.

VALUE CONFIDENCE AS WELL AS COMPETENCE: Being confident about something mundane should never be your objective in life. This simply means that learning the act of confidence while producing poor results is not something anyone should be proud of. When you work on being confident, you should never forget to work on your competence as well. Producing quality content should be your priority as an influencer, while having faith in your own ability to produce good content should come next.

OVERCOME YOUR FEARS: In this life, we were born with only two types of fears: the fear of falling and fear of loud noises. Every other fear in life comes with adulthood and human development. If you ever want to hold your head up in the sky and become really confident in life, you have to overcome any kind of fear you have. Some people are scared of meeting new people, addressing a large audience, or even the fear of expressing their opinions publicly. Although the advent of social media has made it possible for a lot of people to hide behind cyber walls to express their opinions confidently, you still need to master the act of being confident physically. You need to learn how to address an audience confidently. "I try as much as possible to avoid eye contact while addressing an audience, but I end up looking above their heads and losing the attention of my audience while communicating." If you battle with this kind of stage fright, you need to overcome your fears by giving yourself a pep talk before facing an audience.

DISCOVER YOUR SENSE OF HUMOR: If you ever feel like no one understands you while you're expressing yourself, or you ever feel like you are not getting the right vibe from your audience, or your audience isn't flowing along with you, you should use humor to grab their attention. This lessens the tension in a gathering and makes everyone want to listen to you. While using humor, you should also learn to fake confidence in order to appear more confident. If you pretend to be happy, you will become truly happy. Laughing can also help you release endorphins and help you become more at ease and confident.

ACTIONABLE STEPS ON HOW TO BE CONFIDENT

The chapter explains how you can boost your confidence and become really successful in life with the following steps.

• Your first step to becoming a very confident person is to work towards your goals every day. When you take a step closer to your dreams every day, it makes you feel more fulfilled and confident in life.

• Never stop learning if you really want to become confident. Being informed and knowledgeable will help you stay confident.

• Make sure your vision is really clear in order to stay confident and successful.

• Do not give room for negative thoughts or negative people if you want to become confident. Throw negative people out of your life if you really want to become successful and confident.

• Get rid of your fear of making mistakes as this fear only clouds your sense of vision and makes it easy to doubt your own abilities.

• Do not allow a place for doubts in your heart if you want to remain confident as this only clouds your sense of vision.

• Celebrate your little achievements if you want to become really confident. Your gratitude with little achievements will help you achieve greater things as well.

• Get advice and commendations from your role models if you want to become confident.

• Keep a list of your achievements in order to keep you on track when you lose faith in your own abilities.

• Combine confidence with competence in order to be successful.

• You have to overcome your fears in order to be really confident.

• Lastly, you need to discover your sense of humor to maintain your confidence and liven up a boring gathering and conversation.

CHAPTER EIGHT: HOW TO MAKE COOL CASH ON YOUR INSTAGRAM

*H*ow to make cool cash on your Instagram account.

Instagram was originally created as a part-time project by Kelvin Nystrom when he was learning to code along with Mike Krieger. Instagram was launched in the year 2010 when 2500 users showed up on the first day. The real reason for the creation of Instagram was for the sole purpose of picture taking and storytelling. However, anyone would agree that Instagram has now gone beyond that selfie-taking app and has indeed become a great way to make money. For some people, Instagram is that app that kills boredom and helps you see what your favorite celebrities are up to as well as an app that helps you keep up with new trends. While a whole lot of people waste so much data on keeping up with celebrities on Instagram and waste a whole lot of time drooling over the pictures of their "celebrity crush," some other people are busy cashing out cool dollars on Instagram. This is because they have decided to monetize their Instagram account by profiting from their large follower base. You can also choose to be one of those influencers who are making it big on Instagram. All you have to do is to have a large follower base and have great engagement on your content. This simply means you have to learn how to influence and reach a lot of people. Now, let's see ways you can actually make cool cash on Instagram.

Promote affiliate products: Regardless of the industry you are in, you can actually look for phenomenal products you could promote on platforms like CLICKBANK or basically become an Amazon associate by earning commissions while promoting products of your choice which are suitable to your niche. Affiliate marketing, the process of receiving a commission or percent by promoting other company's products, has been proven to be a very beneficial tool for influencers and for everyone in the online business generally. Of course, you might be wondering what this is all about; if you are new to this idea, you do not need to worry. You will be fully equipped with knowledge on how to promote affiliate products after following the guidelines in this chapter. Affiliate marketing basically means you have to endorse a product to your audience and readers using custom tracking links, and then get a referral charge every time someone makes a purchase through your link. There are quite a whole lot of ways to promote affiliate products, and I will try to give a detailed explanation here in this chapter. Although the idea of promoting affiliate products is to make money, you should be very concerned about the needs of your audience, and how you can assist the people who want the product or service you are hoping to promote. You can use a social media campaign for the promotion of your affiliate products; this has been proven to be an effective tool in reaching a lot of people. All you need to do is include links of the product you are promoting in your bio. Instagram doesn't allow you to create links outside your bio, which means that you can only create one link at a time. Several product companies usually run affiliate programs; you can always sign up for one of these programs, get your own unique tracking link, write reviews about such products, or come up with creative, marketable content while you input your custom link in the post. This company automatically pays you when someone visits their website or purchases a product through your referral link. You need to understand that as an affiliate, you are the one who makes marketing happen by promoting the brand and convincing prospective buyers to purchase products from the companies you promote. Being an affiliate has to do with creating awareness and advertising a particular product. As an influencer who already has a large follower base, affiliating is one great way to monetize your Instagram account, because you do not need to own a product before you can make money from creating awareness through your unique links. However, in order to not lose the trust you have built with your audience, you need to be aware of the pros and cons of a certain product before endorsing and recommending to your audience. This is because as an influencer, you are a trend setter, and your audience looks up to you as an inspiration in your niche; they take your recommendations seriously and you should never jeopardize or take advantage of this trust by recommending bad products to your audience. You have to find out if the product is meant for them and also find out if the product you are recommending is of high quality and easy to use. You should also try to know if the product is worth buying through other users of the product. You could also try the product yourself to determine if you should recommend it or not. Do not ever give dishonest reviews about a product just for money, because you might end up losing the interest and the trust of your audience.

Promote brands and services through sponsored posts: Since Instagram ranks 7th on the list of the top 15 most popular social networking sites, you can make cool money on

Instagram by promoting brands and services through sponsored posts. In order to partner with certain companies, you can start pitching to brands and charge depending on the number of followers you have. A lot of influencers charge $10 for 1000 followers while some other people charge according to the number of likes and comments they get. You can reach out to smaller brands or less competitive brands for a start. You could send the sponsors of your choice a direct message through email explaining how you love their brand and let them know the kind of ideas you have for a collaboration. Sending an email can sound a little bit old fashioned, but it is a way to ensure your message gets read and doesn't get lost unlike direct messages. You should send a pitch letter in the email stating who you are, what you do, and how you would be a good option for the brand. You should write a pitch letter like this if you have no idea of how to write one:

Hi,

My name is Lois, and I run an Instagram account (@Lois Jordan). My account focuses on fashion and staying trendy, based on my related experiences as a qualified designer. The people who follow me are mostly female, and they are mostly between 18 and 25 years of age, which seems like a perfect match for the audience your audience targets with marketing. I currently have 50,900 followers and a 100% engagement rate on my posts, and I have also been nominated for the best designer award twice. I think there's an opportunity for us to benefit each other, and I would like to propose a partnership. Here are my initial thoughts on how that might look: (the idea of posts, payment terms, timeline, etc.) I anticipate your reply soon if you think my proposal might be something of interest for your brand.

Thanks for your consideration.

Lois Jordan

This pitch letter is just a sample to help direct you to request for sponsored posts.

SELL YOUR OWN PRODUCTS: One great way to monetize your Instagram account is to open a business page for a product you sell and convert your followers to your potential customers. In order to do this, you have to snap real quality, attractive pictures, and take advantage of the ability to tell stories on Instagram by including very convincing captions to your product. A lot of people also make great money from drop shipping as well on Instagram. You can reach lots of people on Instagram, and it's quite easy for influencers especially to market their own product, because they already have a large follower base who trust them and believe so much in them.

SELL SHOUTOUTS: Making shout outs for money is a great way to monetize your Instagram account. All you need to do is post other people's accounts, products, or services on your own Instagram account to boost other people while charging a fee for doing this. Generally, when you have lots of followers and a high rate of engagement on your Instagram account, a lot of people will reach out to you for a shout out, because they want you to share their products and services with your own audience in order to reach out to more people.

Actionable steps on how to monetize your Instagram

The first method on how to monetize your Instagram is to promote affiliate products by creating awareness through referral links in your bio. You get paid when people go through your unique link to purchase certain products from the brands you are promoting

The second popular method to make money on Instagram is to partner with certain brands through sponsored posts by writing convincing, creative, and strategic posts on your page in order to convince your audience to patronize such brands.

The third method to make money on Instagram is to sell your own product by either having an online store or simply opening a business account.

The last method is to charge people for making shout outs for their content, product, or service to help get them noticed by your own audience.

CHAPTER NINE: HOW TO GET FAMOUS AS AN INSTAGRAM INFLUENCER

Reaching stardom as an influencer can be a little bit frustrating and time consuming. The fact that you are sure you are way better than a whole lot of other influencers who are making it big on the 'gram can be really annoying. I mean, you know you've got what it takes, you know the tricks, you have good and captivating content, yet you are just not getting the fame you deserve. While it can be self-fulfilling to have your name pop up on every popular platform and be really popular for what you do, every influencer wants to get noticed when they walk into random restaurants, shopping malls, and even cinemas, as that "interesting influencer" on Instagram, and the feeling is an undeniably beautiful one. You just want to be notable for being exceptional, and it's not too much to ask.

However, you must understand that "fame" and "influence" are two different words entirely. Influence is the ability to affect, control, or manipulate something or someone—the ability to change the development of fluctuating things such as conduct, thoughts, or decisions, according to the *Oxford Dictionary*—while fame is basically the state of being famous or well-known and spoken of. Why am I giving the definitions of these words? Can you tell the technical difference between these two words and what point I'm driving at? Well, the point I'm trying to make is that being an influencer has a lot to do with changing and shaping the thoughts of human beings. Since the human mind is not a toy, it requires a lot of work and energy to influence; this means that your major objective as an influencer shouldn't be "getting famous," it should be "influencing the human mind in the right way and doing that effectively with the right content." You can get famous while impacting and influencing the human mind at the same time. It only takes certain tricks and methods to get this done. This is not to say that you are not doing the right thing already, it only means that you have to up your game by sticking to certain rules, techniques, and methods to get this done. Adhering to the following rules will get you on your journey of being a global influencer. Now sit back, get yourself relaxed, and ensure every method in this chapter is strictly digested, understood, and well implemented. You really can't wait to be that influencer everyone looks forward to seeing and have people fall head over heels for you, your brand, personality, and content? Then you have to follow the rules laid down right here:

Ensure your bio is updated: Ensuring your bio is filled sets you up on your journey to "global domination." No exaggerations here; well, maybe just a little bit of an overstatement, but indeed, having your bio filled actually gives someone who is visiting your page for the first time an idea of what you do. Make sure your bio isn't boring, but captivating. If you will be using Instagram for your influencing career, not having a personalized bio makes your Instagram account incomplete. Making a unique bio has to do with using the limited space you have to come up with something really creative and hilarious, which is going to be the first impression your followers need to have about you in order to hit the Follow button. You start by introducing yourself, what you do, your location, and the purpose of your Instagram account. You can also use one of your favorite quotes or simply draw attention through an original quote or short write-up. Your bio should also include a very nice picture of you or what your page is all about. Ensure the picture you choose is of a very nice quality and captivating enough to attract visitors to your page; you could also use a logo that stands as an identity for your brand. Since Instagram only gives you 150 characters to fill up your bio, you have to ensure you make it an attention-grabbing one of really catchy words and by being succinct and straight to the point. You can also check on popular Instagram users and take a clue from their bio. You can also use emoji to describe what you do if you just can't come up with something creative or unique.

ALWAYS INCLUDE CAPTIONS: One thing that makes people famous on Instagram is the ability to be really expressive. Although you can promote your brand through visual skills, it is really good to include captions in your posts. If you do not want to write lengthy descriptions, you could just say a few things about the pictures instead of leaving captions out totally. The use of captions can make you famous, because it is what tells your audience how you think, how your mind works, and the kind of message you have to pass across. You should use interesting and creative captions, but you do not need to use too many clichés or boring chat. Your caption can be hilarious or just to give a little bit detail on your photos and the events and circumstances surrounding the pictures.

USE PHOTO EDITING APPS TO MAKE YOUR PICTURES AWESOME: Everyone will agree with the fact that having good pictures on your Instagram page can actually grab your audience's attention. While it is essential to snap quality pictures with a good camera or a very nice iPhone, you can also edit your pictures with several picture apps to make sure your pictures are really attractive. For unknown reasons, pictures with the "No Filter" tag actually appear to have more likes than filtered pictures on Instagram. It would be nice to use other photo editing apps to edit your pictures if you do not want to use any of the filters. There are quite a number of photo editing apps you should try. They include Photoshop Express, Snap Seed, Camera, Afterlight, Visco Cam, Nour Photo, Color Splash, etc.

GEOTAG YOUR PICTURES: When you take pictures at certain locations, you should try to include your location in your caption by tagging your location in the picture. This will allow your picture to show up when people search for that location you have tagged. You should do this often, especially when you are visiting a new place; it will enable the people in the same geographical area to find your account easily.

DEVELOP A PERSONAL HASHTAG: Coming up with your own personal hashtag can earn you some fame or popularity. First, you ought to know what a hashtag is—it is simply a word that comes after a pound sign (#). You must have seen a lot of popular Instagram influencers or celebrities who use quite a lot of hashtags. The idea behind the use of hashtags is to make it easy to find your page and make your content pop up under this popular hashtag. This is not to say that you should use hashtags that aren't related to your niche or suitable for your content. However, you should only try to ensure that you use more hashtags than less, and also develop a very unique hashtag for your brand that makes it easy for people to find you. For example, if you are known for baking, and your brand name is Katie, you could use the hashtag #katiecookies or #katiecakes until the hashtag sticks. This is exactly how to create personal hashtags. Hashtags also increase your chances of having visitors follow your account as it makes your page pop up when these hashtags are clicked on. One thing you should also notice is that in the example of the hashtag I gave above, #Katiecookies, you should never punctuate your hashtag when using them; all the words in your hashtag should be deliberately unspaced. Your hashtag should also not be a long sentence—just a couple of words will do. The highest number of hashtags you can use on Instagram is thirty-two, and you shouldn't exceed this limit, even though it is advisable to use quite a lot of hashtags to ensure your page gets noticed. After creating your own hashtag, you should ask your family and friends to promote your hashtag by using it, and you should also try to promote it yourself by using it on different social media sites.

DO NOT FORGET THE POWER OF STORY-TELLING: This book puts a lot of emphasis on the act and power of storytelling. The truth is that life itself is a story; to become famous as an influencer, you are working with the human mind, and there's just no better way to do this than to tell relatable, captivating stories. You want people to be really in love with your content? Then let them see themselves in the stories you tell; they want to be educated, inspired, and entertained. The power of storytelling will help you achieve this through a straight-from-the-heart kind of experience. Everybody has a story. We all have good stories, heartbreaking ones, and sorrowful stories, and since we have a lot of people in this world, do not be surprised that somebody somewhere is going through or has gone through what you have been through as well, and this is exactly where originality comes in. When you tell authentic stories, people will lend you a listening ear (the attention you need) and will be compelled to tell you their own stories (the engagement you crave from an audience). They will look forward to reading more stories from you (and here's the fame you want). Social media has given you a voice; don't be afraid to tell your stories in an entertaining manner. If you think you are not a good story writer or teller, you could just take an experience from the previous day or a recent event. What do I mean? How about what happened at the grocery store the other day? That friend you ran into and pretended didn't know you because of a new difference in class and status? Well, I'm not saying this exact thing happened to you—all I'm saying is you could pick something out of your daily experience; there are lots of people out there who can relate to being snubbed by a friend. When you share yours, you give them an opportunity to stop and pay attention to you and relate their experiences by leaving a comment. They just instantly feel like you already have something in common, because they were able to relate to you on a personal level. Your story might be a humorous event or the use of memes, but the idea of storytelling has never been such a bad idea.

WORK ON YOUR FLUENCY: While expressing yourself is a very wonderful idea, you should try to express yourself correctly and fluently. Do not use a word if you are not sure of the meaning of such words; make sure your sentences are grammatically correct and ensure they convey the exact meaning you want to pass across to your audience. A lot of people get tired of reading incoherent sentences with ambiguous meaning. You don't want to be known for using the wrong words, so build your vocabulary and ensure you communicate the right way. Nevertheless, your content shouldn't be about grammar itself, it should be straight from the heart and deeply expressive. This basically means you have to combine originality with fluency in order to interest your audience and grab their attention. You will discover that a lot of popular people on Instagram are very good at expressing themselves correctly and fluently.

BE GENUINELY INTERESTED IN WHAT YOU DO: If you really want fame as an influencer, just like every other career, you need to be really involved in what you do. Let people see how invested you are in what you do. Know what drives you and find your drive and inspiration. Let your passion show through your content and be interested in everything that comes with being an influencer. Find your own voice and use it to your own advantage. Don't be afraid of expressing yourself and your passion, rise beyond limitations, and let people see what you really want to offer this world. When people see the passion that drives you, they become genuinely interested in your dream and help you rise to stardom as an influencer.

BUILD AN ENCHANTING FEED: If you want to become Instagram famous, one of the first things you should never forget is the need to build an enchanting feed. What do I mean by an enchanting feed? I'm not asking you to get a Cinderella magic wand to build an enchanting feed; all you have to do is to make sure your feed is really fascinating and attractive. There are so many ways to do this. Nobody likes to visit a page that's filled with a cluster of "eye sickening" themes. You do not want people to hiss and consider your page degrading on their first visit, do you? Well, I'm sure nobody does. When you get wonderful and eye-catching themes for your Instagram page, it encourages you to post more often and brings you more followers. You should use colored grids to make sure your feed is beautiful. You could come up with ideas on how to mix these colors by changing them row by row until it's colorful enough to attract your audience. You can also use puzzle grids where the squares or posts all fit perfectly like a jigsaw puzzle. This is where you get to use different squares that overlap, spread together where your pictures overlay, or cross over into the various squares. These grids allow you to be really creative while making your Instagram feed just as enchanting as possible. You can also try "tiles;" they allow you to mix a variety of images and written posts as well. You can also use a vertical grid; this vertical grid allows you to post your pictures on vertical lines, it's really intriguing, , and creative. One other distinctive grid you should try to make your feed enchanting is the triangle grid; it puts your pictures in each triangle and gives your feed a whole different look. Some people do not think it necessary to have a good-looking feed, but it is really important to have one. It gives a really wonderful first impression on your audience and also gives them the impression that you took your time to create something this beautiful for your followers. It is a great impression and shows your creative side while boosting your image brand. The beauty of Instagram is that it allows you to express your visual ideas and creativity. One great way to take advantage of this is by building an enchanting and fascinating feed with the use of themes.

CREATE CONTENT OF SUBSTANCE: The major reason behind your content should be "impact." In order to make impactful content, you must ensure your content doesn't lack substance. You have to ensure that quality supersedes quantity when making your content. All content must be beneficial to your audience.

BUILD CONSISTENCY: If you want to become famous as an influencer on Instagram, you cannot be on and off kind of person. You should practice the act of consistency and make sure you post every day. Do not make your followers or audience wait a long time before hearing from you. You do not need to post just anything, which makes no sense, because you want to stay relevant, but you need to post as often as possible. It is impossible for your audience to forget you when they hear from you often.

USE THE CTA METHOD: The CTA method basically stands for CALL TO ACTION. It means that you need to state in clear terms what you really want from your audience. You could say something like "drop a comment if you like this," "double tap," or "drop a caption." An example of a CTA is the use of "teasers;" you can tease your audience by writing a suspense-filled short story halfway while you make them wait for the next part by saying things like, "Coming soon…" or, "Anticipate tomorrow…" You can also encourage your followers to tag their friends in your post. You can also say, "Turn on your post notifications…" You should also use arrows to direct your audience to a link. Your call to actions shouldn't be demanding or commanding; you should ensure there's something beneficial for your audience in some CTAs. For instance, you could say "First 20 people to comment will get a follow back from me," or, "Turn on your post notification, so you don't miss the giveaway I will be doing by a particular time."

NEVER BUY FOLLOWERS: No matter how desperate you are for fame, you should never buy followers. Getting famous can get really tough out there, especially if you are just starting out, and you are just not getting your desired attention and fame. Don't fret. Don't force it even if the soaring figures seem like a good idea, you should never do it. This is because the engagement you get from fake followers is "zero." It doesn't boost your engagement, and it makes it so easy for anyone to know that you have actually bought followers when you have just 15 posts and you already have 1 million followers. This will not earn you fame; it will act as a great turn off on the part of your audience. Remember, influencing has to do with the human mind, and the last thing you want is to come off as a shady or dishonest person to your followers. If you feel you must buy followers, do not make it obvious at all; just a little boost will do. I personally do not recommend buying of followers because the figures just don't add up.

USE SHOUTOUTS: One sure way to get new people to check out your page is through the use of shout outs. What is a shout out? Just as the name implies, it is the act of introducing another person's page and what they do on your own Instagram account. You can pay to get popular people on Instagram to mention you on their own account and share you with their own audience. If these people like what you do on your page, they will instantly follow you. This method is a widely used one among Instagram users and can help you get at least one hundred new followers who are interested in your content. An estimate of about 300 million people use shout outs as a means of advertising every month. You can use it, too.

SET YOUR ACCOUNT PUBLIC: If you are interested in getting famous on Instagram, you should never make your account private for any reason; this is because it is really hard for new people to find you and even your hashtags if you do not make your account public. More so, a lot of people instantly lose interest in your account if it's private. Influencers are meant to be public people, and if you want fame as an influencer, setting your account private should never be on your mind. Sometimes, you might notice a certain comment on a popular page on Instagram, and you are intrigued; you want to get to know this person more and what his or her account looks like. When you click on the name and the account appears private, you instantly return to your destination and forget about the page. Well, other people might be persistent, but I know a lot of people who will leave rather than follow a private account.

GET PUBLISHED: Another amazing way to earn yourself fame on Instagram is to get your account published by popular online magazines.

ENGAGE YOUR AUDIENCE: No matter what kind of method you use to make your account popular, it is very important to engage your audience. When new people visit your account, the only way to keep them interested is to leave automated messages that serve as a welcome message to your audience. You should reply to comments on your page as often as possible, follow accounts of some of your followers you like, and interact with your audience and make them feel at home on your page.

COMMENT ON OTHER POPULAR ACCOUNTS: You should try to comment on popular Instagram accounts who have so many followers on their accounts, especially those who have a similar niche with you. When you comment often on these popular pages, there's a one-hundred-percent possibility that you may find new followers who are interested in your page. You do not need to spam other people's accounts with fake compliments just because you want to get noticed. This would probably not work out well as other people may sense your desperation and just not follow you back. Your comments should be really genuine, intelligent, and intriguing. People love really clever people and would want to follow you to find more intelligent posts or write-ups from you. You shouldn't be known for bullying people or leaving hateful comments just for attention. I personally know a friend who got most of his 250k followers from commenting often on popular accounts. He was really known for his consistent, intelligent comments, and people would always wait for his remarks and even search for his comments on certain posts. A lot of people would even tag him and wait and anticipate his observations. This was because he showcased his intelligence and made people value his opinion. You can also give this a try and comment often on popular Instagram accounts to reach out to more people.

EMBRACE YOUR INSECURITY: If you really want to become a famous influencer, you have to learn how to embrace your insecurities, get over your fears, and don't be afraid to dream. A lot of people will try to put you down and make you feel like you are not doing the right thing, but you just have to ignore the naysayers and concentrate on being the best version of yourself.

ACTIONABLE STEPS ON HOW TO BECOME FAMOUS AS AN INFLUENCER

Now, you have read and can fully understand what it takes to become famous as an influencer. You are motivated to set the ball rolling, and you just can't wait to get on the nearest fame bus and become the next popular influencer. All you need to do is to follow the methods mentioned in this chapter. These methods can be summarized into the following:

• Make sure your bio is filled and updated; your bio has to be an advertisement for your page and convey the purpose of your page. Consider it a short introduction for your audience.

- The second method you should never forget is the use of captions and not pictures alone to express yourself to your audience

- Make sure your pictures are well edited by using any photo editing app of your choice to increase your picture quality.

- Make sure you tag your location in your pictures. This is called "geo-tagging," and it will make it easier for your account to gain visibility

- One other thing you need to do to become famous as an Instagram influencer is to develop your own personal hashtag which sets you apart from other people and gives your brand the uniqueness it deserves.

- The next step is to use the power of storytelling to your advantage. Tell relatable stories to entertain, educate, and influence your audience positively.

- Work on your grammatical structure and ensure you communicate fluently without being ambiguous.

- Be passionate about what you do, and let the world see how genuinely interested you are in what you do.

- Build an amazing and captivating feed with the use of attractive and unique themes.

- Make sure your content is impactful and highly beneficial to your audience. Everything you do should revolve around the quality of your content.

- Being consistent will also make you famous over time because consistency will definitely put you out to the public sooner or later.

- Use Call to Actions to state exactly what you want from your audience, telling them in clear terms how they need to go about it.

• If you want to become a famous influencer, you should never consider buying followers as this only gives your audience a negative impression about you.

• You should also use shout outs if you want to become popular on Instagram; all you need to do is pay for one or ask other people to give you a shout out on their accounts.

• Never set your account private if you ever want to become popular on Instagram as this only makes it difficult for people to find you.

• You should also get your brand or content published or featured in popular magazines or other online publications.

• Do not ever take the attention of your audience for granted; you should continuously engage your audience in several ways.

• One amazing technique mentioned in this chapter is to comment regularly on popular accounts to help you reach new people and become prominent as an influencer.

• The last step is to overcome your fears and embrace your insecurity if you desire to stay focused until you have reached your goal.

CHAPTER TEN: GROW YOUR COMMUNITY

Grow your community through paid advertisement.

THE MAGIC BEHIND GIVEAWAYS.

Since the advent of several social media platforms, a lot of business organizations have gained online and global prominence through online marketing, and several marketing strategies have been used by several business-minded people and online marketers to promote their brands and showcase their businesses to the members of the public. In the recent years, when influencers found their "voice" on social media, they have come up with different ideas to reach out to more people and have tried to reach a place of global prominence as well. A whole lot of influencers have grown their community through the use of paid advertisement. What is a paid advertisement? Just as the name implies, it has to do with creating awareness about the existence of your brand with the members of the public through a mode of payment. Our major focus of paid advertisements in this chapter is the use of a "giveaway." What does giveaway mean? And how does it count as a paid advertisement? Well, everyone is already familiar with the concept of "buy one, get one free," and almost everyone is fascinated with the idea of an ongoing promo or having a chance to win exotic things through the purchase of a relatively cheap product.

I remember going to a nearby store as a kid to buy a packet of sweets every day, because I stood the chance of winning a bicycle, face cap, or a small-sized scooter. Although I never won, not even a pencil or any other little thing, they could have at least compensated me. I still bought this packet of sweets every day anyway, not because I liked it; I remember giving them out to my friends so many times, but the idea of winning a prize fascinated me, and I would beg my mom to let me buy.

This is exactly what happens every time there's a prize attached to something; it increases the sales margin and leverages the desire of the potential buyers to buy more. Whether you are an influencer or just a businessman or woman, the magic behind giveaways is a great one that every influencer should put to use once in a while. Not only does it help you gain more followers, it serves as an advertisement for your brand and puts your content out there, especially if you promote your giveaway on very popular websites. The following tips will help you host a very successful giveaway:

COME UP WITH A GIVEAWAY THEME: A lot of influencers who have hosted giveaways often decide on a particular theme or reason. Giveaways are actually fun and engaging, because you get to interact with your audience and also get to see the hilarious and creative part of your followers, especially if the contest is a challenge type that requires your audience to be really creative and super dramatic. You can decide to host a giveaway to celebrate hitting a certain number of followers, celebrate your birthday, your business, or wedding anniversary or simply because you just want to give back to your audience in a way. If it's your first time hosting a giveaway, you do not need to be afraid or nervous. Once you have come up with a reason or theme, the next thing is to determine what you are giving out and the rules involved in the contest.

DECIDE ON THE RULES: A lot of influencers come up with certain rules for their giveaways. You should state in clear terms the rules guiding your giveaway and what qualifies and disqualifies applicants for participation in the giveaway. Your rules should be based on the purpose behind your giveaway. If you would be using Instagram for your giveaway, one rule you must adhere to is "the statement of release." A lot of people who use Instagram are unaware of this rule, but it is a very essential rule you ought to keep in mind when hosting an Instagram giveaway. The rule states that you have to include the fact that "this giveaway or promotion is not sponsored by Instagram or associated with Instagram in any way." You also need to ensure that "by entering, participants are above 13 years of age." By doing this, you have released Instagram of responsibility and agreed to Instagram's terms of use. These rules were laid down by Instagram to ensure that your promotion is carried out legally without you breaking any government rule applicable to your area of residence or country. The rules you set personally on your giveaway should depend on what goal you are trying to reach. If your goal is to get more followers, you should make sure your participants follow you and tag more people to follow you as a requirement to participate in your giveaway. On the other hand, if your goal is to increase your brand prominence and visibility, you should ensure your participants repost your Instagram contest pictures and tag their friends in the comments under the picture. This giveaway strategy will definitely help make your brand visible. Other rules include posting a creative video that helps build your brand or coming up with a creative comment in order to win a particular prize.

SELECT A PRIZE: When hosting a giveaway, you have to decide on the kind of prize you want to give out. A lot of people make the mistake of choosing prizes that are in no way related to their niche; what this does is to make your new followers leave after they have gotten the prize, because they were only interested in the prize attached to the giveaway. If you want to host a giveaway because you need more followers, the best way to go about your giveaway is to give out a prize that's tied or related to your niche. What do I mean by this? If you happen to be a sports influencer, it would be a bad idea to give out an iPhone or give out a pair of heels. The only new followers you would gain may only be interested in your iPhone and have no passion for sports in any way. On the contrary, the best gifts to give out as a sports influencer are track suits, sports shoes, or anything related to your niche as a sports influencer. If you happen to be a fashion influencer, you also have to come up with a gift that's suitable to your niche. If you have a product of your own or render a particular service, you could give it out as well, it will serve as an advertisement for your brand and help your brand gain visibility as well. Whatever niche you are involved in should determine the kind of prize you give out to the participants of your giveaway or contest.

CHOOSE A DEADLINE: If you ever host a deadline, you have to come up with a deadline that states how long the giveaway lasts. Some people believe you can actually get more followers by ensuring your giveaway lasts for a long time; however, the best way to host a giveaway is to set a limited time. This is because you don't want to go bankrupt providing gifts for a lot of people. Having a limited time limits the number of participants. You are the one who decides the deadline you want for your giveaway. The maximum time should be seven days. When deciding the deadline of your giveaway, always consider the difference in time zones and your international audiences; you should understand that some of your followers do not live in the same country as you, so you have to ensure your deadline is clearly stated and easily understood by your international audience. You should also consider the shipping expenses and delivery fee if you would be delivering the gifts to winners in different time zones.

CREATE AN EYE-CATCHING POST: If you have decided on a theme, a prize, and a deadline, the next thing is to come up with a post that clearly states the requirements and the prize attached to your giveaway. The post should be well-designed and colorful with the giveaway and prize attached written in bold letters. You should also include the image of the prize attached to the giveaway. The requirements should be clearly written in the caption section to enable your participants know exactly how to get into the contest. You might be wondering why a giveaway is often referred to as a contest; it is often referred to as a contest because you have to compete with several other people to emerge as a winner. After creating a fascinating post, the next thing is to set a reminder that tells your audience just how long your contest lasts for.

CREATE A REMINDER: You need to set a reminder for your audience; this tells them when the entry for the giveaway ends. You can decide to remind your audience every day after the announcement of your giveaway or few days before the giveaway ends. You should state the requirements for your giveaway again in your reminder, using a similar picture with the first giveaway post you made.

SELECT A CREATIVE HASHTAG FOR YOUR CAMPAIGN: One of the things you should never forget when hosting a giveaway is the use of a campaign hashtag that makes it easy to promote and locate your giveaway. After coming up with a hashtag, you should ask your contestants or entrants to use this hashtag when reposting your giveaway post, commenting, or tagging, depending on the rules guiding the giveaway or stipulated in the giveaway criteria. Since a lot of people enjoy competing in giveaways while others love free stuff, using a campaign hashtag for your giveaway will help you create better recognition for your brand and also help you with social media momentum or energy. When your participants use your unique campaign hashtag, it can help your giveaway go viral, which will be to your own advantage as it certainly helps you gain more followers and help your brand become really visible.

YOU CAN ASK PEOPLE TO SPONSOR YOUR GIVE-AWAY: There are several people out there who are interested in making their brand visible and increasing the number of their followers. These people may be interested in sponsoring your giveaway or teaming up with you to raise money for the giveaway. All you have to do is to include the name of your sponsor or sponsors (brand or individuals) in your post and ask your participants to follow them in order to get the prize attached to your giveaway. You can also sponsor other famous people's giveaways in order to reach more people and create awareness for your brand. A lot of people use this strategy (paid advertisement) to gain more followers.

· · ·

PROMOTE YOUR GIVEAWAY: Having a wonderful give-away idea is important but failing to spread the word about your giveaway will not make your giveaway worthwhile. You need to come up with great strategies to promote your give-away. This is the only way your efforts in hosting your giveaway do not amount to nothing. No matter how creative and fun your giveaway is, you still need to let people know about it. You don't need to rob a bank to promote your giveaway. The only thing you might have to spend is your time and innovation. You can promote your giveaway on all of your social media platforms as well as by emailing, which is a very personal way of reaching out to people. It is a good idea to notify your subscribers, followers, or audience via email after 24 to 36 hours of launching your giveaway. This is advisable, because it affords you enough time to correct mistakes and be sure your giveaway is worth promoting. You can also reach out to some of your audience who is not yet aware of your giveaway to notify them and encourage them to participate or join the contest. You can add a personal tone to your email by addressing the recipients of your mail by their names. You can also drop a link in your email to ensure your audience gets the correct information and makes it easier for them to join the contest with a click. You should also encourage your audience to refer other people and spread the news to their friends and family about the giveaway. Referrals are very trusted, and they are also an example of "'personal marketing." Most people would refer your giveaway to the people who are most likely going to be interested and increase the number of your follow-ers. You can also promote your giveaway on Facebook, which is the largest social media platform on the internet. Facebook will help you reach a lot of people at once. You will definitely have no regrets boosting your giveaway on Facebook. You can also promote your giveaway on different sites for free; these sites can be seen below.

. . .

REDDIT.COM: Reddit is one website out of several that allows you promote your giveaways for free. Reddit was founded by Steve Huffman and Alexis Ohanian in 2005, and they passed the site on to Condé Nast publications in October 2oo6. The site, however, became an independent subordinate of Condé Nast's parent company in 2011. Reddit currently has its headquarters in San Francisco. As of March 2019, the site had been able to reach 542 million monthly visitors, which makes it the sixth most visited website in the United States and the 21st most visited in the world. It is an American social news aggregator and web content ranker where registered members are allowed to submit their content such as links, text posts, and images, which are then voted up or down afterwards by other registered members. Reddit allows you to post links to your giveaways on the app and promote your giveaway to millions of users without having to pay a dime. You have nothing to lose; once you get the Reddit app from Google Play store, you should be on your way to creating wonderful awareness and visibility for your brand.

ONLINE SWEEPSTAKES: OnlineSweepstakes.com, which is also known as OLS, is one of the biggest websites for promoting your giveaway for free. It is a sweepstakes directory offering that lists several giveaways and affords you the opportunity to exchange tips with other users of the website. Online-Sweepstakes was originally created in the year 1997 and has been one of the greatest online sweepstakes sites ever since. The community is a reliable one with hundreds of users across the globe. The website allows both users from the United States and across the globe. As a registered user of the site, you have the liberty to promote and include your giveaway by filling an online form which requires your data. Although, you can use OnlineSweepstakes free of charge, most of the most attractive features are only available only with a paid participation.

CONTESTCHEST: ContestChest.com is also one of those websites where you can promote your giveaway for free. All you need to do is to register as a member and enter your contest on the website to promote and reach more people.

CONTESTGIRL: ContestGirl.com is a directory for US and Canadian giveaways and sweepstakes. All you need to do is fill in your details in the form provided on the website, include the rules guiding your giveaway, and how to locate your giveaway as well as the social media platform used for the giveaway. Contest Girl is one website you can trust for the promotion of your giveaway.

GIVEAWAYMONKEY: This website, GiveawayMonkey.com, is especially open to promote your brand and giveaway. The website has been in existence since the year 2012 and has proven to be reliable and trustworthy so far. This site, just like other aforementioned sites, allows you to promote your giveaway and create awareness for your brand and help you gain prominence and visibility.

THEPRIZEFINDER ThePrizeFinder.com is also a free website that allows you post your giveaways for promotion. The website boasts of several positive reviews to their name since they started a long time ago.

SWEETIESSWEEPS: This website presently has about 8837 members and has been in existence since 2008 when the website first emerged for the sole purpose of helping people win giveaways and sweepstakes. The website, just as its slogan says, has actually "helped a lot of people win the things they cannot afford." This site is currently active on various social media platforms, including Facebook and Instagram. They help you promote your giveaway on their platform by posting the pictures and details of your giveaway on their platforms as well as share links to your page on their platforms.

GIVEAWAYFRENZY: This website was launched in the year 2015 and has since been used by lots of people for the promotion of their giveaways. You can try GiveawayFrenzy.com by entering your giveaway on the website for promotion and brand visibility. This website helps you showcase and advertise your giveaway to a lot of people as it is a trusted site that has about 100 listings per day.

Other popular websites you could use for your giveaway promotion include the following:

- **OZ BARGAIN.COM**

- **SWEEPSTAKES.COM**

- **TOTALLY FREE STUFF.COM**

- **MIX.COM**

- **GIVEAWAY PROMOTE.COM**

- **WIN A SWEEPSTAKE. COM**

- **CONTEST CANADA. COM**

- **EMPEROLA.COM**

• **SWEEPSTAKE.COM**

ACTIONABLE STEPS ON HOW TO HOST A SUCCESSFUL GIVEAWAY

• Come up with a theme for your giveaway: you could host a giveaway to celebrate an event or for other reasons

• Decide on the rules guiding your giveaway

• Select a prize you would be giving out to your audience

• Ensure there is a deadline for your giveaway

• Make sure your giveaway post is eye-catching

• Create a reminder

• Create a unique hashtag for your contest

• Ask people to sponsor your giveaway

• Promote your giveaway on your social media platforms or other websites you could use for free, like any of the mentioned ones.

CHAPTER ELEVEN: MISTAKES YOU SHOULD NEVER MAKE

*M*istakes you should never make as an influencer.

Just like every other business, career, or job, there are certain rules you must adhere to as an influencer. Although a lot of popular influencers have made these mistakes, you should learn from their mistakes and not repeat the same mistakes as well. In this chapter, I will be explaining in detail the kind of things to look out for as an influencer and what other popular influencers have to say about these mistakes and how to go about avoiding them.

INABILITY TO SAY NO: One common mistakes most upcoming influencers make is the inability to say *No* to brands that do not have anything in connection with your niche. Once you have reached a certain number of followers as an influencer, a lot of brands would want to collaborate with you, because they know you have quite an influence over your audience. You might get really excited, especially if it's a huge deal, but you have to consider if this brand has anything in common with your brand or is in any way related to your niche. You might be tempted to accept this deal, but you should never do it if it's going to confuse your audience and appear totally different from what you usually do. Remember you would never have been popular without the help of your audience, so you should really not be afraid to say no to brands that do not have anything in common with your niche. A lot of popular influencers like Lilach Bullock and Cameron Conaway have recorded their biggest mistakes as "saying yes to everything." You should try to look out for this mistake and avoid it at all costs.

INCONSISTENCY: One other problem a lot of influencers encounter is the inability to be consistent. This happens when you try to be everywhere, have a presence on multiple platforms, and are unable to post regularly. Well, if this is your problem, you are not alone; other popular influencers like Sheryl Plouffe and Brian Carter have made this mistake as well and have recorded it as one of the biggest mistakes they have made. The truth is that lack of consistency actually sets you back and can make it really hard for you to be successful. However, Brian Carter advises upcoming influencers to concentrate on only a few platforms they can handle in order to not lose audience interest along the line and end up being inconsistent.

GIVING UP ON THE THINGS THAT EARNED YOU FAME: Brian Hart and Ian Brodie once admitted that the biggest mistake they have ever made as influencers was "losing sight of what got them fame in the first place." A lot of influencers seem to make this mistake; it's more like you are just not trying to impress your audience anymore once you have gotten the fame you have always wanted. This is where passion comes into play: if you love what you do so much, you will never stop trying to impress your audience. Regardless of how you started out, whether you earned your own fame through dancing, using memes, or highly creative content, you should never give up on these things. There's a ninety percent probability that your audience might get sad if you stop doing these things, and you might start losing followers. I personally know an influencer friend who became famous by posting her dance videos on her platforms; by the time she had hit 9 million followers, she gave up on dancing all together and concentrated on advertising for several brands instead. You can already guess what happened to her. She lost about 50,000 followers because her page became really boring, and by the time she realized what was really happening, it was almost too late. You don't want to be in this kind of situation, so you have to make sure you do not get too relaxed after getting your desired engagement and followers. I know you might find it difficult to do, but you have to embrace and hold on to the things you did that earned you fame in the first place.

NOT KNOWING YOUR OWN VALUE: When brands start reaching out to you to help them create awareness for their brand, you might be offered stipends, and they might offer to pay you less than you deserve; do not be scared of telling them your own terms and what you will accept. Chelsea Krost also revealed his biggest mistake as an influencer was "not having a conversation with his brands." A lot of brands might give you the impression that they already have quite a number of other influencers to reach out to. However, you do not have to be scared of negotiating with them. Influencers like Chad Pouliot and Warren Whitlock have made this mistake and advises upcoming influencers not to make a similar mistake. Likewise, do not ever be tempted to take on more projects than you can handle; consider your own terms before the terms of your brand. It's a win-win for both parties.

NOT PUSHING HARD ENOUGH: A popular influencer named Charlene Li once recorded this as her biggest mistake as an influencer. Charlene Li explained that she has never and would never regret the things she did, but she does regret the things she *never* did as an influencer. This is a mistake you should never make as an upcoming influencer. Do not be tired of trying, even if things don't work out as planned. If you do not push hard enough or take risks, you might never be known or ever cut your teeth as a popular influencer.

UNDERMINING THE POWER OF COLLABORA-TION: Chirag Kulkarni once said that the biggest mistake any influencer can ever make is "not collaborating with other influencers." This is particularly true for some recent and upcoming influencers; quite a number of them do not know how essential it is to collaborate with other influencers. What this does is to enable these influencers share their own audience with you, which would definitely benefit you in so many ways.

CHOOSING FAME OVER IMPACT: Influencers like Dan Knowlton and Jonathan Dana advise upcoming influencers not to ever make the mistake of choosing fame over impact or trying to become famous before becoming an influencer. What does all this mean? These two great influencers are only trying to lay emphasis on the fact that your aim should not be to become famous. On the other hand, your goal should be "making an impact in the lives of your followers or audience." If you ever want to become famous as an influencer, you should never be more interested in becoming famous instead of being a qualified content writer. The goal should be how to make your audience benefit from your content as an influencer; having this at the back of your mind will definitely earn you the fame you deserve as time goes on.

TAKING ON A BRAND FOR PERSONAL REASONS: Evan Michael revealed his greatest mistake that he regrets so much was "taking on a brand for personal reasons." Evan explained that he knew from onset that this brand in question had absolutely nothing in common with his niche, but for personal reasons, he agreed to the contract. He later revealed that this decision turned out to be a wrong one as it was neither beneficial to his audience nor the brand. One thing every influencer should learn from Evan's mistake is to never take on a brand whose idea or theme doesn't conform with your niche.

IGNORING THE INTEREST OF YOUR COMMUNITY: According to Deirdre Breakenridge, the biggest mistake any influencer can make is "not having the interest of your community at heart." This means you should always consider the interest of your audience before making any decision. If you have to partner or strike a deal with any brand, you have to overlook the prize and consider how this brand will benefit your audience first. Do not put the lives and safety of your audience at risk for money as this would definitely jeopardize your relationship with your audience and destroy the confidence and trust they have in you. Do not ever make the mistake of putting money above the interest of your audience as the consequences may be greater than you can ever think.

. . .

INABILITY TO BE RELEVANT: Gerry Moran once said that the biggest mistake you can ever make as an influencer is to stop being relevant. This is a common mistake amongst influencers who have collected some followers for themselves. After some influencers have worked hard to an extent, after getting enough recognition, they automatically stop being relevant and cut back on the things they used to do initially. You should never find it difficult to stay relevant or make it hard for your audience to locate you after getting attention.

GIVING UP ON LEARNING: Grant Cardone admitted letting his ego get the better of him because everyone looked up to him as an influencer and as someone with a very high IQ, and he gave up on learning all together. Grant Cardone admitted this was his biggest mistake ever and encourages other influencers to never stop learning. Do not ever feel like you know enough. Stay educated; keep learning every day to keep you on your toes, so you do not lose your relevance. Remember, quite a lot of people love highly informed influencers; you could lose your audience if you stop being informed or give up on learning.

NOT DOING ENOUGH RESEARCH: This is somehow related to the previous point but also very different in a way. Holly Pavlika, an award-winning creative marketing and social media veteran once noted that this has been her biggest mistake as an influencer. You do not want to make the mistake of not doing enough research and putting out misguided information. Remember, your audience members are not dummies; some of them have enough knowledge in certain fields and can always call you out when you provide incorrect information. In order to avoid making this mistake, Holly Pavlika advises you to do your homework really well.

TRYING TO PLEASE EVERYONE: Jaime Masters, who is a business coach, author, and speaker revealed that this has been one of her biggest mistakes so far. The truth is you need your audience to be on the same page with you, just as you need to have their best interest at heart. However, one mistake you should never make is "trying to please everyone." Human beings are naturally insatiable; you cannot please everyone at the same time, no matter how hard you try. Some people will not see things your way, and this shouldn't be a problem or cause you to give up. The most important thing is your confidence in what you do and the fact that you are not breaking any rules or doing anything wrong. You shouldn't obsess over what everyone thinks about you or your brand.

WORRYING ABOUT AUDIENCE SIZE INSTEAD OF ENGAGEMENT LEVEL: Jeff Epstein and other influencers who have made this mistake would tell you how much this mistake has caused them in their careers. This is exactly what the buying of followers boils down to. When influencers, especially the newbies, opt for buying followers, it is because they worry about the size of their audience rather than the level of engagement. This should never be your priority; you should never choose your audience size over engagement level. To avoid this mistake, do not ever buy followers and never take your audience for granted. Engage your audience and make them feel special by establishing a cordial and personal relationship with them. This is what sets you apart from influencers who are majorly concerned with their size of audience.

NOT MAKING YOUR TERMS CLEAR: Jill Schiefelbein once said, "not getting everything in writing" is the biggest mistake any influencer can ever make. This means that you have to make your terms clear when signing deals with brands if you do not want to be cheated. You should also read contracts page by page before signing them in order to avoid any future problems. Do not ever make the mistake of taking on a deal in a rush without first assessing what the brand does, nor fail to understand the rules and regulations entrenched in the contract. Never assume the brand knows even the smallest of information; you should write them out in clear terms regardless of how obvious they are.

NOT HELPING OTHER UPCOMING INFLU-ENCERS: John Boitnott verified that this has been one of his biggest mistakes so far. This happens a lot especially when you have made it big in the industry—you tend to forget how you started out by refusing to carry other influencers along with you. Always remember, you never know who is going to be the next popular influencer in the industry, so you should never look down on beginners or you might regret it in the future.

GETTING POLITICAL: John Steimle revealed that this has been one mistake he has learned as an influencer, and John Merodio also admitted making a similar mistake by posting the picture of a politician on his social media platforms as a result of a project he was working on at the time. The popular influencer said he was called out for doing this because a lot of his audience weren't in support of the politician in question. Although Merodio felt bad and apologized, he would never repeat the same mistake ever again. This mistake is one you should run away from as an influencer unless you want a backlash from your audience. Do not ever post anything related to political affairs or talk about it on your personal platforms. It is the easiest way to cause a rift amongst your audience. Your goal should be "bonding with them," not tearing them apart from you. It's completely normal for people to have different political views, and do not be surprised some people are quite passionate while others are politically apartheid and might lose interest in you or your brand for your choice of political candidates. Always keep in mind that getting political is one of the biggest mistakes than can ever be made by an influencer.

NOT WRITING COMPELLING CONTENT: When asked if he would ever take back anything he has done so far as an influencer, Larry Kim replied saying, the only thing he regrets so far is the fact that he could have written more compelling and quality content. Do not be surprised; most influencers only work on the quality of their content when they are just starting out, and after getting some fame, they fall back, and the quality of their content diminishes. However, this can be a big mistake on your part because the influencing world is quite competitive, and everyone is trying to outdo other people in the same field. The very moment your audience sees a reduction in the quality of your content, they might lose interest in your brand and content as a whole.

NOT TAKING OUT TIME TO CULTIVATE YOUR OWN IMAGE: Laura Pena Antencio once explained how she got so engrossed in helping other people create an image for themselves and build their audience's engagement, that she totally neglected her own self and brand. Some influencers make the mistake of forgetting to help themselves while getting carried away with helping other people. Do not get this twisted; you should help other people, however, concentrating too much on others might rub off on you in a way. It doesn't make you selfish. It only means you have to take the time out to build up yourself and your confidence and how to relate with your audience. In Laura's words, you should "focus more on you and take care of your business."

HAVING TYPOS OR GRAMMATICALLY INCORRECT WORDS: Lisa Sicard believes one of the biggest mistakes you can make is writing content that is not very well structured or grammatically correct. You do not want to come off as an incompetent writer by making mistakes or typos in your write-ups every time. Although mistakes are inevitable sometimes, you should try to make your content more impressive by having someone who has a great command of the English language proofread it before publishing.

NOT HAVING A COMPLETE BIO: Mary Smith believes every influencer should have a complete bio that clearly states that you offer influencer marketing services. This sounds obvious, but some influencers do not feel the need to include this in their bio. However, you need to know that some brands might not notice you if you do not include this clearly in your bio. You have been taught how to fill your bio in the previous chapters; you should ensure your bio clearly communicates your ideas and niche to your audience and brands alike.

NOT ANALYZING NUMBERS: Several popular influencers like Kat Sullivan admitted making this similar mistake. Do not ever underestimate the need to analyze your data or numbers. In order to know exactly what your audience wants from you, you should analyze your data to see the content they are sharing, the content with the highest likes and comments, as well as the countries your audience lives in. There is a chapter earlier in this book that teaches you how to use Google Analytics. You will benefit greatly from using this method to analyze your data. Failure to do this will leave you uncertain about the things your audience really needs to know as well as their areas of interest.

NOT SHARING POSITIVITY: One of the biggest mistakes you can make as an influencer is your inability to spread positivity. Keith Keller attests to this notion. Society is already filled with enough negativity, chaos, and madness. It would be so wrong to not use your power to influence the human mind to spread positivity. To avoid making this mistake, ensure you spread hope, love, and positivity throughout your content. Let your content become a "go-to" place for comfort and hope. Your platform should help your audience ease the tension in their lives.

FAILURE TO REMAIN AUTHENTIC: Meghan Ducile says you will be nipping yourself in the bud by failing to remain authentic. You should never make this mistake, because your audience can instantly tell when you are not being original. Do not try to copy someone else's technique; you should try to register your own voice and techniques into the mind of your audience by concentrating on doing your own thing and trusting your instincts and intentions. As long as you are passion-driven, there's nothing wrong in trying to be yourself or simply being original.

HAVING NEGATIVE ROLE MODELS: Nadya Khoja, who is a very popular influencer, noted this as her biggest mistake. If you have role models who are popular for doing the wrong things, choosing such people to be your role model will be a mistake you'll wish you never made. Role models who do not support you or your decisions or who often make you feel less of yourself by making you want to quit should never be your role models. Some people also have role models who let their fame get into their heads by refusing to mentor upcoming influencers. These types of people should be avoided at all cost as they are only interested in dimming your light.

AIMING FOR PERFECTION: Rebekah Radice's regret as an influencer is "aiming for perfection." Never try to be perfect at all costs. Most popular influencers are not even perfect; they just try to do their best and leave the rest. If you understand the fact that perfection is underrated, you wouldn't aim for perfection; you would only try to be good at what you do and deliver your best to your audience without stressing to be perfect.

This particular chapter was written to help you learn from other influencers' mistakes and help you make the best decisions in your influencing career. Here's a summary of the aforementioned mistakes you need to watch out for:

¬ Inability to say no; never be scared of saying no.

¬ Stopping the things that earned you your fame; you should never give up on the things that earned you fame in the first place.

¬ Not knowing your own value; do not be scared of demanding more from brands if the need arises.

¬ Not pushing hard enough; the greatest regret you can have as an influencer is wishing you had done more.

¬ Not collaborating with other influencers; the earlier you start reaching out to other influencers for a collaboration, the better.

¬ Choosing fame over impact; work towards impacting the lives of your audience instead of running after being famous.

¬ Taking on brands for personal reasons; never work with a brand that has nothing in common with your niche for any reason.

¬ Inability to stay relevant; never stop being relevant no matter how popular you already are.

¬ Giving up on learning; never stop learning no matter how old or how educated you are.

¬ Not doing enough research; always get your facts straight and avoid misguided information.

¬ Trying to please everyone; never try to satisfy everyone. Different people will always have different opinions about you and your brand.

¬ Worrying about audience size instead of engagement level; your priority should be the level of engagement you have and not the size of your audience.

¬ Not making your terms clear: always ensure your terms are clearly stated in your contract to avoid any sort of misunderstanding in the future.

¬ Not helping other upcoming influencers; never forget the days of your early beginnings by refusing to help other upcoming influencers. Remember, you started out like them.

¬ Getting political; never include your political views in your personal platforms.

¬ Not writing compelling content.

¬ Having typos or grammatical errors in your content.

¬ Not having a complete bio.

¬ Not analyzing numbers.

¬ Not spreading enough positivity.

¬ Inability to remain authentic.

¬ Having negative role models.

¬ Aiming for perfection.

CHAPTER TWELVE- INFLUENCER MARKETING

In this chapter, we will be looking at the theory of influencer marketing as well as the relationship between this strategy and traditional social media marketing. What is influencer marketing? Basically, influencer marketing is like a fusion of ancient and modern marketing strategies: replacing the idea of using celebrity endorsement with the use of people who have an influence over their target audience through content-driven marketing campaigns. The major difference between influencer marketing and celebrity endorsement is that the outcome of these marketing campaigns is often a collaboration between the brands and influencers involved. A lot of brands have held these successful influencer marketing campaigns and a lot of brands are still into it. Although it's simple to envisage a celebrity teaming with a company to endorse a product, that's nothing compared to a collaboration with an influencer. A lot of people talk about influencer marketing, and you can't help but wonder what this is all about. This shows you how "trendy" the idea of influencer marketing is today, unlike several years ago when other marketing strategies were used for brand awareness and promotion. In contrast to celebrities, influencers can actually be anywhere. Anyone can be an influencer. They don't have to be actors, musicians, or super models to become influencers. However, what makes them really influential is their huge followings on the internet and social media platforms. An influencer can be a popular photographer on Instagram or a relationship blogger who is well read on any social media platform. Every industry has several influential people—you only need to find them. They are usually recognized by their huge follower base, and that's the target audience desperately needed by brands.

The misconception behind influencer marketing?

Every brand needs to understand the fact that influencer marketing goes beyond finding just anyone with a large follower base and giving them an amount of money to say something good about your brand. This is something celebrities would do, but influencers, on the other hand, are individuals who have taken enough time to establish their own personal brand, and they reach a number of audience members who believe and have great trust in their recommendations. Influencers know how hard they worked for every follower they have and would never take the love of their audience for granted; they are often not interested in quick payouts. **Influencer marketing is also not about quick payouts.** It uses the same methods as social media and content marketing that doesn't involve the selling of products directly. It goes way beyond that; it has more to do with building an impact and exhibiting credibility and leadership within your industry. It involves aligning with whatever services you render.

.   .   .

With social media marketing, it's a steady process of building your relationship with the ideal audience who would vibe along with the content you provide. Although influencer marketing gives a brand a chance to strike a chord in the hearts of an influencer's audience, it doesn't come on a platter of gold. This is because, as a brand, in order to get influencers to see things your way, you should try to earn their trust and make them respect you. Now how do you do this as brand?

What you should never do as a brand when hosting influencer campaigns:

Using the same technique when dealing with different influencers: You need to understand that various influencers have different rules and principles. What works for Influencer A may not work for Influencer B. When you have this in mind when dealing with influencers, it will help you to avoid generalizing.

Considering only the fame of the influencer: When selecting influencer, a brand should never be too concerned about the fame of an influencer; what you need to ask yourself is if the influencer can help you reach your target audience and if the influencer is the best to help you bring your goals to reality.

Never compare traditional social marketing with influencer marketing: Influencer marketing is very different from traditional social marketing in the sense that social marketing only created an identity and awareness on a select few platforms, and over time, they reached out to more people and were able to determine their loyal users. What does this mean? They were able to determine the potential customers who liked, shared, and spread the word about their brand, or customers who wrote reviews about their products. These kinds of users were never taken for granted; instead, the brand would build a relationship with them through engagement and personal responsiveness and attention. These sets of people were encouraged to spread the word about the brands and products as a marketing strategy. Influencer marketing, on the other hand, tells us how essential it is to spend your time as a brand in direct marketing to influencers whose policies you are already familiar with; they work in a similar industry and have carved a niche and reputation for themselves. The problem with the approach of the traditional social media marketing was that a lot of the users whose loyalty the brand depended on just could not reach enough of an audience. They only had a few friends and associates whose preference might not even align with the brands in question. This was a problem on the part of the brands using these people as they just weren't getting the attention they craved. You can already imagine the result of the approach; it was "disastrous" because there was barely any change in the brand's awareness creation. The strategy of influencer marketing, on the other hand, emphasizes spending your time on people who have quite an influence over their audience and would leverage the desires of their audience to buy your products without having to manipulate anybody. It can also mean building or creating content that's exclusive to attract these influencers. While it's the influencer's audience that's the definitive prize, the target market for these brands is the influencers themselves.

CONCLUSION

The concept behind this book was to let you know all there is to know about being an influencer. The very first chapter about communicating passionately was written to help you find passion in what you do. The other eleven chapters were also written to get you to become the wonderful influencer you have always wanted to be. The actionable steps in the chapters of this book should make the message in every chapter clear and summarized, to enable you to put each and every point to a very good use.

My objective is that, after reading this book, you will be fully equipped on what you need to do and what you shouldn't do as an influencer. The goal is not just to be a regular influencer, but to be the best version you can be. Good luck!

FREQUENTLY ASKED QUESTIONS ON HOW TO BE AN INFLUENCER.

Right here, we have compiled some questions people regularly ask about being an influencer:

• **Who is an influencer?** An influencer is a person who is involved in the business of impacting the lives of their target audience in any field or industry they have chosen. They are experts at what they do and often consider the interests of their audience before making certain decisions.

• **What is the difference between a brand ambassador and an influencer?** The difference between an influencer and a brand ambassador is the way they both treat their brands and how they are compensated. A brand ambassador is someone who is paid for representing the voice of a brand or advertising the brand in question. While an influencer is an individual who ensures that the idea of a brand resonates with their audience, they put the interests of their audience first before making any decision or signing a deal with any brand.

• **Is influencer marketing a good marketing strategy?** Yes, influencer marketing is an awesome strategy that every brand should try. It has worked for several brands; it should work for your brand as well.

• **Do you need to be active on all social media platforms to be an influencer?** No, you don't have to be active on all social media platforms. However, whatever social media platform you have chosen, to be an influencer should be your priority, and you should endeavor to be very active on such platforms.

• **How often should an influencer post on social media?** It depends on what appeals to you as an influencer, but you need to be consistent and post as often as you can.

• **Are influencers paid?** A lot of influencers are paid, depending on the kind of deals they sign with certain brands.

The End.

✽ Created with Vellum

www.ingramcontent.com/pod-product-compliance
Lightning Source LLC
Chambersburg PA
CBHW061544050726

47593CB00002B/897